W9-DJE-248

LEARNING TO CONTROL STRESS

LEARNING TO CONTROL STRESS

M. W. BUCKALEW, JR., Ph.D.

Illustrations by
NANCY LOU GAHAN

RICHARDS ROSEN PRESS, INC.

NEW YORK, N.Y. 10010

10-12-88

Published in 1979, 1982 by Richards Rosen Press, Inc.
29 East 21st Street, New York, N.Y. 10010

Revised Edition 1982

Library of Congress Cataloging in Publication Data

Buckalew, M. W.
    Learning to control stress.

    1. Stress (Psychology)   I.   Title.
BF575.S75B82   158′.1   79–11708
ISBN 0–8239–0496–2

Manufactured in the United States of America

For
Barry
and
Elizabeth

Preface to the Revised Edition

Since this book was published in 1979, new research has disclosed information which has been incorporated into this new edition.

About the Author

Dr. M. W. (Buck) Buckalew does research into human stress and teaches courses in Stress Control in the Education Department of St. Lawrence University, Canton, New York. He frequently offers a Saturday morning course called Biofeedback and Athletics for high school juniors as well.

Before going to Canton in 1974, Dr. Buckalew spent six years teaching English and coaching various sports in North Carolina, Arizona, and Wyoming high schools. He now spends considerable time away from the university, making presentations on Stress Control throughout the United States and Canada, or competing in 26-mile marathon races.

"Some people think I'm crazy to do as much running as I do," he admits, "and they might be right! But I've found that doing a 26-mile race is much like doing well with stress control.

"You have to take good care of yourself in training. And you have to calm yourself during those first miles when you feel like sprinting but you know that if you do you won't be around at the finish.

"Stress control is similar. You have to learn to take good care of yourself if you're going to finish strong on an examination or perform well in a job interview. I want young people to learn to manage their stress levels so they can do really well on tests, in sports, in their social lives, in everything—and learn to enjoy these challenges, too."

Preface

In one sense, this book is written for high school students. But in another sense, it is written for everyone. The stress control techniques you'll read about in these pages have nothing to do with a person's age. Whether you are 15 years old or 85 years old or somewhere between the two, these techniques ought to prove equally useful for you.

But the examples I have used throughout the book to illustrate the use of stress control techniques are taken from high school life—the stresses of test-taking, for example, or of athletic competition, or of job interviewing, or of college-entrance interviewing, or of teen-age social pressures. That is the sense in which the book is directed toward high school students. Anyone else, however, who has ever been a high school student should have no trouble understanding these techniques and how to use them well.

As you will see, the idea is not merely to control stress. We can all avoid stress simply by staying in bed all day. The idea is to learn to "manage" our stress levels so that we can do what we have to do as *well* as we would like and so that we can enjoy meeting life's challenges as well.

I am convinced that people can have their cake and eat it, too. I am certain that students can make top grades (by managing their stress levels skillfully and, of course, by studying!) and that they can learn to be relaxed, happy, and healthy in the process. But I've said enough for now. Start reading and decide for yourself.

Contents

LEARNING TO CONTROL STRESS

CHAPTER I

What Is "Stress"?

Tension. Fear. Nervousness. Anxiety. Any of these words will do to give you an idea of what I am going to be talking to you about. This book is designed to help you to take a look at your insides and to find out what happens in there when you're faced with something you think of as stressful. It could be just about anything: dating, for example, or going out on the court for a basketball game against a cross-town rival, or the next big examination that will determine your grade in a course, your chances of getting a job you want, or the possibility of getting into the college of your choice.

A lot of doctors and other medical people are paying attention today to stress in the adult population. Your parents and grandparents, your teachers, your principal, your coaches, the manager of the supermarket, the cop on the street corner—all these people are the objects of a great deal of study and concern. Why? Because adults are constantly getting sick or even dying at least partly because they don't know how or when to relax. They think they must be tense or "psyched up" all day long in order to do a good job at whatever they're trying to do. They may think they have no choice about their nervousness and tension. They may just say, "Well, I'm a very nervous type of person."

Adults are often surprised to discover that a good deal has been learned in recent years about how to handle the stresses of living. It has become clear that there *are* choices a person can make as to whether to be a "nervous type" or not. For those who think that being continually psyched up is the path to success, there is the news that they may very well do a better job if they learn to avoid being uptight all the time. They may then not only feel better but also think much more clearly, especially when they are under pressure. As a bonus, they probably would not get sick so often, and they would almost certainly live longer.

At your age you are not likely to become really ill just from stress. Your body is still too fresh and young to cave in completely just because you're not handling your own pressures as well as you should. You probably have quite a few years to go before your doctor would begin to notice certain health problems related to stress.

That does not mean, however, that stress is not important for you right now. For one thing, if you learn a few things about handling yourself better while you are still in your teens, you will have a much easier time as you grow older in dealing with the pressures of your job, your marriage, your children's problems, and so on.

For another thing, if you take time now to work on stress control, you may find that life as a teen-ager is considerably more pleasant. Not that this would solve all of life's problems, of course. But think about yourself. How often do you have headaches? How often is your stomach upset? How often are the butterflies in your stomach so bad that you can't really enjoy a date, can't really look forward to a contest, or find yourself feeling absolutely terrible as an examination approaches?

And how about your performance on that examination? Are you so uptight that you score much lower than you really should?

Well, that is what stress can do to you right now, long before you reach the age where it becomes a "medical problem."

CHAPTER II

Stress and Performance

Recently I invited college students to come to my laboratory to take part in an experiment. They came one at a time and were hooked up to machines that are designed to tell how stressed—nervous, anxious, scared—people are. Then they were asked to solve some fairly difficult arithmetic problems in their heads. Those who were very stressed solved the problems very poorly. Those who started out stressed but learned to relax by doing some of the things I suggested to them began to solve the problems much better. Not only better than they themselves had done prior to relaxing, but better than the ones who were not taught to relax. They actually were able to think more clearly just by doing certain things to reduce their stress levels.[1]

Even more recently I visited a class of high school students each Friday for 15 minutes and gave them a few stress control ideas. After only six weeks of this (a total of 90 minutes of class time), these students were doing noticeably better on examinations.

I did not ask the students to practice at home the steps toward stress control. You can see, then, that they worked only a short time—a total of an hour and a half—on stress control steps. Even so, their exam scores came up.[2] Stress control for test-taking is not hard for most students to learn, and it takes little time. However, as with anything else, the harder you work

---

[1] M. W. Buckalew, Jr. "An Experimental Study of the Relationships between Anxiety and Cognitive Functioning." *Forum on Open Education,* 1977–78, Vol. V. pp. 21–25.

[2] M. W. Buckalew, Jr. "Effects on Public School Students' Examination Scores of Learning Stress Control Techniques—An Experimental Study." *Forum on Open Education,* 1978–79, Vol. VI, pp. 77–79.

on stress control and the more practice time you devote to it, the better you are likely to get.

Each spring I teach a Saturday morning course for high school juniors on stress and athletics. Usually I have about 15 boys and 15 girls in the class. In athletics, of course, it is important to learn to psych up and psych down, depending on the sport and the situation. For example, playing good defense in basketball demands that you be very psyched up in order to stay with your opponent and play him or her very tough. But what about shooting a free throw? If you can't psych down and truly relax for the free shot, you will miss most of the time.

At one point in this course, I introduce the students to rappeling. That is a mountain-descending technique in which you let yourself gradually down a mountain (or the side of a building) using ropes and buckles. You should be very psyched down to do this because it requires almost no muscular effort. But can you be relaxed—unstressed, unafraid, not tense—when you are hanging 40 feet above the ground? Again, by using a few simple stress control ideas, most (not all!) of these high school juniors have been able to maintain their usual heart rates and normal stress levels under these frightening circumstances.

As you watch professional athletes, television entertainers, musicians, and other outstanding performers, you observe people who have learned to control their stresses and so to increase their levels of performance. You can see that, even under great pressure, they have taught themselves (1) to think clearly, (2) to make good decisions, and (3) to recall the things they need to remember (as you must do on your exams)—for example, a quarterback remembering the details of the game plan while 50,000 spectators are shouting at him, a musician remembering exactly what his or her cues are and how the lyrics should be sung while a national television audience watches and listens, an actor or actress recalling precisely how the dialog is to be delivered while critics judge the performance for their newspaper stories.

Do not forget that all these excellent performers have studied

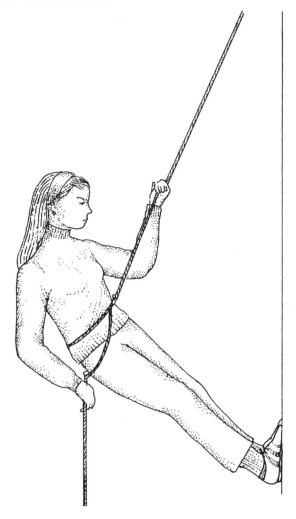

Rappeling.

before they were "tested" by their opponents, their audiences, and their judges. Stress control is no miracle. It will not help you recall facts that you have not learned in the first place. It will not help you understand a chemistry experiment or a Hemingway novel that you never took the time to study or read before the exam was given. It will not help you do well in an interview for a job or for acceptance into a college if you have not spent time finding out what the job or the college is like, and finding out about yourself by thinking about your own strengths and weaknesses, your likes and dislikes.

I am talking about learning to control your tension so that you can show your teachers (or coaches or employers or university admissions officers) exactly how much you do know and understand. For example, if you practice stress control ideas, you should be able to walk into any test perfectly confident that you will be able to write down everything that you have studied. But you must not mislead yourself into thinking that you are going to score higher than you deserve to—stress control *and* good study habits will produce the results you want. One without the other will do very little for you.

CHAPTER III

Symptoms of Stress

The following is a list of things many people find themselves doing or experiencing when something stressful is coming up in their lives. Which do you find in your own?

1. Overeating
2. Taking tranquilizer pills ("downers")
3. Losing appetite
4. Irritability
5. Headaches (including back of neck and upper shoulders)
6. Insomnia (difficulties in getting to sleep or staying asleep)
7. Diarrhea
8. Constipation
9. Cold hands
10. Sweaty hands
11. General tiredness
12. Stuttering or uncontrolled speech
13. Hyperactivity (unusual, uncontrolled bursts of "nervous energy")
14. Colds and other minor illnesses
15. Aches and pains (other than those listed above)
16. Difficulties with concentration

It is certainly true that you may find yourself very stressed during examinations, contests, dates, or performances without necessarily experiencing any of those problems. But one of the first steps in trying to do a better job with stress control is to become aware of exactly what happens inside you when you are stressed. "Listen to yourself" as the next stressful event in your life approaches. What are your brain and body trying to say to you?

As I move now into the specific steps you can take in order to control your stress, I want you to be thinking about which of these steps could be used to help you deal with items on the list, and which could be used to deal with your stress problems that may not make that list at all, such as simple poor performance on exams, or in athletic and musical contests, or on college and job interviews. You will probably find that most of the steps (which I am going to call "techniques") can easily be used in either type of situation—either to help you deal with general stress symptoms or to help you deal with your specific "performance problems."

CHAPTER IV

Breathing Control—Stress Control Technique #1

Try this. Press your index finger into your neck, just beside your Adam's apple. Do you feel your pulse? Now count the number of heartbeats that you feel during the next minute.

That number is your normal pulse rate. Most people's hearts beat about 70 or 80 times a minute. If you are in pretty good physical condition, your heart rate may be considerably slower— maybe even below 50. A strong, well-conditioned heart beats more slowly than a less well-conditioned one.

Now force yourself to breathe deeply and rapidly for the next minute. After you have done this, press your index finger to your neck again and take your pulse while you continue to breathe deeply and rapidly for another minute. What was your heart rate this time? If you are like most of us, the rate was probably quite a bit higher—maybe 10 to 20 beats more than the first time. That's perfectly normal. When we increase our intake of oxygen, our hearts must pump harder to distribute the oxygen to the cells all over the body that are reached by the bloodstream.

Do a final experiment. Sit up in your chair, feet flat on the floor, back perfectly straight. Let yourself calm down after the hard work of breathing so deeply for two minutes. Next, begin to watch your chest and stomach move as you breathe normally. After watching yourself for a few minutes, try this. Each time you breathe out, pause for two seconds before you take your next breath. Try not to make that next breath a deep one—just a normal one. Don't make yourself uncomfortable doing this. Just relax and see how it feels to take this two-second pause between

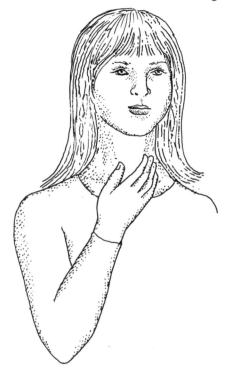

Pulse-counting.

normal breaths. Finally, continue to breathe with the pauses and count your pulse for another minute.

What was the count this time? Most people find that when they control their breathing in this way their heart rate drops several beats below normal. Your heart is being given a chance to relax because you are putting less demand on it to circulate the oxygen to your body.

Some students have asked me why holding the breath would not be the quickest way to slow the heart down. But if you hold your breath your body soon becomes alarmed that no oxygen whatever is coming in. An alarmed body is exactly what you do not want for controlling your stress. An alarmed body will respond with an increased heart rate, not a slower one. What you must learn to do is to reduce your oxygen intake without leaving your body short of the oxygen it requires.

When you become stressed—upset, angry, scared, frustrated—a number of things begin to happen automatically in your body. There is a name for this: "the fight-or-flight response." Your body is getting cranked up to fight an attacker (a saber-toothed tiger?) or to run away from the attacker (a very slow saber-toothed tiger?). Of course, in the 20th century you are seldom called upon really to fight someone or something, or to run away, and this is especially true of things such as examinations. An exam cannot be fought with your fists, nor can it be run away from—not if you want a decent grade in the course, or a chance at a job, or a place in a university you wish to attend.

By learning to keep your heart rate down through practice at controlling your breathing, you can become very effective at turning off the fight-or-flight response whenever you wish. Sometimes you will not want to turn it off, such as when you are about to run the 100-yard dash in a track meet or when you want to beat up the neighborhood bully. But the fight-or-flight response will not help you to take examinations nor to be poised when you have to make an oral book report in front of the class. Nor will it help you to be "smooth" on your next date—friendly, relaxed, thoughtful, and mildly energetic (that's "mildly energetic" compared with fleeing that saber-toothed tiger).

In fact, it will do just the opposite. The fight-or-flight response may make you have to struggle to think clearly. It may make it almost impossible for you to recall facts rapidly and accurately. It may make decision-making (as on a multiple-choice exam question) far more time-consuming and puzzling than it should be. It may make it tremendously difficult for you to think of anything to say to your date as you ride with him or her to the movie. Your body is getting you ready to fight or run, not to think! You are not going to need much muscle power to push a pencil across a piece of paper, or to speak to a classroom full of your friends, or even to engage in a wrestling match with your girlfriend or boyfriend on the front seat of your car. I mean,

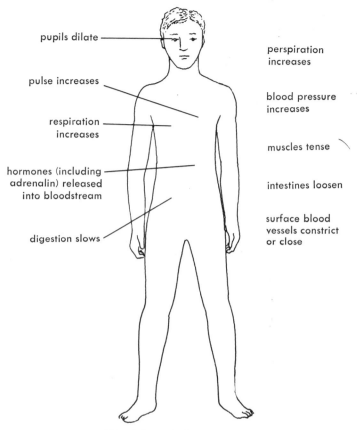

pupils dilate

pulse increases

respiration increases

hormones (including adrenalin) released into bloodstream

digestion slows

perspiration increases

blood pressure increases

muscles tense

intestines loosen

surface blood vessels constrict or close

The fight-or-flight response.

it's not really the kind of wrestling match that requires you to fight with all your strength. At least, I hope it's not!

Some of you are basketball players. Probably most of you have played the game at least a few times, and nearly all of you have at least watched a basketball game at your school or on television. Have you noticed what most good players do when they shoot a free throw? If not, watch closely the next chance you get. This is what you will probably see.

You will see the player who was fouled walk to the free-throw

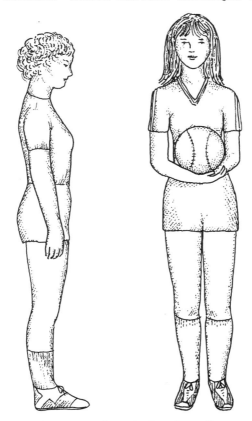

Stress control on the free-throw line.

line and stand looking down at the floor, beginning to relax. You will see the player shake his or her arms and legs slowly, encouraging the muscles to become less tense. If you watch carefully, you will usually see the player take one or several deep breaths and then let the breath all the way out. Only then will he or she begin to eye the basket and prepare to shoot.

This is breathing control. It is exactly what I am suggesting that you should practice doing in all sorts of scary situations, although I want you to do it in a slightly different way. I wanted to call your attention to basketball free-throw shooters to remind you that many people use "stress control techniques" without having the slightest idea that that is what they are doing. If you asked basketball players why they took those deep, slow breaths on the free-throw line, most would probably say something like, "Well, it makes me feel better," or "It helps me calm down," or "It helps me concentrate better." Exactly! These players have somehow learned, probably without ever being told by a coach, that controlling their breathing in this free-throw situation helps calm them down.

Since you have read the first few pages of this chapter, you know precisely why these basketball players feel more relaxed when they take deep, slow breaths. You know that they have forced themselves to stop breathing rapidly, that they have reduced the amount of oxygen they are taking in, and that they have given their hearts a chance to slow down because there is now less oxygen to be circulated through the body. You understand, too, that the basketball player can sense that he or she does not need the fight-or-flight response in order to shoot a free throw. That response may be needed soon, as the player fights for a rebound at the other end of the court. But not now.

Since so many people play or watch basketball, why do you suppose so few people realize that breathing control, if practiced correctly, could help them to control their stresses in *all* the frightening or challenging situations in their lives? Maybe it is because they would feel a little embarrassed to take several deep, slow breaths just after sitting down in a small office at the beginning of a college admissions interview. Well, I think I might feel that way myself. That's one reason why I suggested earlier that you teach yourself to pause for two seconds between normal breaths. In that way, no one will have any idea that you are using a stress control technique.

The other reason that I recommend that you use the two-second-pause method is that it is an even more effective way to reduce your oxygen intake than deep, slow breathing. Both ways work, but I think my way is a little better, and it has the advantage of letting you be sneaky about your stress control.

I have spent about 15 years coaching boys, girls, men, and women in a variety of sports. One of the things you find in sports, of course, is pain, and not just from injuries. Injuries do happen, unfortunately. But pain in some form is part of almost every practice and every game or match, isn't it? Think about all the different kinds of pain: the pain of sore muscles, the pain of gasping for breath, the pain of exhaustion, the pain of losing . . .

I learned early in my coaching life that one of the best things I could do for a player who was in serious pain was to help him or her to control breathing. I remember my first football team, a junior high squad in a small Western town. On one of the first days of practice the team's fullback, after being tackled, rose from the ground and then doubled over in pain, gasping for breath and holding his sides and abdomen. I simply took him aside and talked to him softly, asking him to relax further and to try to make his breathing a little more shallow so that his oxygen intake rate would return to normal levels. In less than a minute his pain was gone, and, after resting a short time and being checked for broken ribs by the trainer, he returned to the practice session.

Had his ribs in fact been broken, the fullback's pain would certainly not have disappeared as a result of breathing control. But I am convinced by now that pain, no matter where it is in the body and no matter what its cause, can always be at least reduced by breathing control and by other stress control techniques that we will study later in this book. Pain, of course, no matter what kind and no matter why we feel it, is always made much worse by fear and the accompanying tension and stress. Controlling the stress reduces the pain. It's as simple as that.

Dentists are becoming very much aware of this. Several years ago I attended a meeting in Toronto, Canada, which was being held to study the subject of hypnosis, especially in regard to its effects on pain. Of about 200 of us at the meeting, over half were family physicians, some were psychologists, and about 60 were dentists. The idea of the meeting was to learn how to speak softly, in a very relaxing way, to one's patients, so that the patient would be able to relax fully. By relaxing fully, the patient controls the amount of stress he or she is feeling. And by doing this, the pain felt in the dentist's chair can be greatly reduced. We were taught at the meeting that, of course, one of the most important things to do when talking to a patient about relaxing was to help the patient become aware of his or her breathing, and to encourage the patient to breathe in a relaxed manner.

Remember the last time you were nearby when a two-year-old child fell down or was accidentally hit with something. Remember the sobbing and crying that just wouldn't stop? Often the sobbing and gasping continue even after you have successfully talked the child into laughing about something. When we see something like this happen, it can remind us of how closely connected pain and breathing control really are. When the youngster is hurt, the breathing goes almost out of control by means of crying and sobbing, often making the child think that the pain is much worse than it really needs to be. As we grow older, we gain the ability to control our breathing when we are hurt, but few of us are ever taught to do that. Instead, we are often taught to clench our teeth, tense our muscles to fight the pain, and maybe even hold our breath in the process. All of this may help us keep from crying in front of our friends, but it is just the opposite of what we should do to reduce the pain itself. Relaxation reduces the pain, not tensing. It is usually far easier not to cry from pain if we take our two-second pauses between breaths, relax our muscles, especially the ones in the throat, and stop trying to fight so hard against something that really can't be fought.

Even though this happened a little more than 20 years ago, I can picture my friend Linwood sitting across the room from me in algebra class, just as if it were yesterday. Linwood had reddish hair and thousands of freckles. (I had tried to count them once when he and I were in the seventh grade, but was forced to give up without ever going beyond one of his forearms.) Linwood was also very bright, a good athlete, and a leader in our school.

But he was not perfect. One day in algebra class he made a remark to our teacher that angered her considerably. She proceeded to scold him severely and at length in front of his classmates.

Linwood was sitting in the front desk of a row on the other side of the room from me, but I was near the front of my row and, since he was turned sideways in his desk to face the teacher, I could see his face clearly. I was amazed and impressed to see that, throughout the entire scolding, Linwood showed absolutely no signs of embarrassment. He simply stared at the teacher, with no nervous smiles, no looking at the floor, and, most impressive of all, no blushing even amid that sea of red hair and freckles. Linwood just looked directly at the teacher's eyes, listened to her tirade, and then went back to his work.

Later I told him that I was really impressed by his ability to handle the situation without apparent embarrassment. He looked both pleased and surprised that I had studied him so closely during the incident, and then he asked me if I knew how he kept from blushing. I confessed that I had no idea, and he told me that the secret was breathing control. I wasn't sure what he was talking about, so he explained that he had found that whenever he was beginning to feel embarrassed he could keep the blood from rushing to his face by forcing himself to breathe very shallowly—that is, by taking very small, short breaths.

After that I occasionally used the technique myself when I felt embarrassed. But I did not realize until years later that Linwood had discovered for himself an excellent all-round stress control technique, one that could be used in a great variety of situations to lessen stress and tension. When I did realize it, I was surprised that it had not occurred to me before. I should have been able to figure out that Linwood's shallow breathing was reducing his oxygen intake and thereby inviting his heart to continue to pump blood at its normal rate, preventing that awful rush of blood to the face that we call "blushing."

Of course, blushing is not necessarily a bad thing, and I even think it can be beautiful in some females; but I do like the idea of having a choice as to whether or not to blush. I like having choices about everything, in fact. I don't like to feel as if I am being forced to do something, whether it is going to a meeting, or being polite to someone I dislike, or blushing when I don't want to blush. Above all, I do not want to be stressed when I can do something about it. And, after practicing for a while, I have found that usually I can indeed do something about it. For me and for a lot of people I have taught and coached and counseled, breathing control has been a very effective technique in stress control.

Before we move on to other techniques, I would like to tell you of two other real-life examples, then describe in detail how you might use breathing control in a classroom situation.

A couple of years ago one of my university students became pregnant. Since she was not married, she was fearful of talking to her mother about it. She was pretty sure she knew how her Mom would react, and whenever she thought about the scene that would occur she felt highly stressed. The closer the time came when she would have to tell her Mom, the more time she spent thinking about this terrible problem and, of course, she became more and more highly stressed.

Does this sound familiar to you? When something is coming up that you dread going through, do you find yourself thinking more and more about the awful event and consequently feeling increasingly stressed? Remember the stress symptoms I listed in Chapter III? Do you find yourself running into some of those symptoms when you get closer and closer to having to go through with something you have been dreading?

Well, this pregnant student of mine—let's call her Jane— decided that she was going to do better with this stressful situation than she was used to doing in others. She decided to practice and then use breathing control when it came time to inform her Mom of her pregnancy, and also to force herself to think about the problem differently. We will talk at length in Chapter VI about making yourself think differently about problems.

When the time came, Jane controlled her breathing and, she

said, was therefore able to keep her heart rate nice and slow. Jane's body listened to her mind, which was thinking about the problem differently, and her body responded to her careful breathing by maintaining a normal pulse rate, a normal blood pressure, a normal temperature in her hands (because the blood continued to flow through them normally)—and how do you suppose the conversation turned out? I'll give you a hint. Did you know that when you are calm and "together" it helps other people to be calm as well? Think about the last time you saw someone get furious. Were other people who were being yelled at able to stay calm? Or did they look nervous or upset or frightened? Or did they just get furious in return? Notice how seldom people get upset when you tell them something very calmly. If you have never tried this, check it out.

As you have guessed by now, Jane's mother took the news calmly, and the two of them were able to have a long, friendly talk about the baby and about a lot of other things that they had not discussed in a long time. Jane told me she was sure that her ability to control her own stress helped her Mom to control *her* stress, too. That's the way it works many times. But even if Jane's mother had lost her temper and blown up, at least Jane would have been able to control her own emotions and would not have had to struggle with the stress symptoms of headache, upset stomach, and so on.

By the way, did you understand what I meant when I said that Jane's hands stayed at a normal temperature because the blood continued to flow through them at a normal rate? I mentioned in Chapter II an experiment I did in which college students came to my lab and were hooked up to machines designed to tell how stressed a person is. One of those machines reads fingertip temperature. One of the best ways, strangely enough, to measure how stressed a person is at a given moment is to measure the temperature of the fingertips. A high reading of, say, 95 degrees (F) indicates that he or she is very relaxed, with the warm blood flowing smoothly just under the surface of the skin. A low reading of 75 or even 65 degrees shows a lot of stress. When we become stressed, you recall, we experience the fight-or-flight response. As part of that response, the tiny blood vessels just under the fingertips become much smaller—some of them even close up entirely. So, with less warm blood passing just under the fingertips, the surface temperature drops more and more.

You don't need one of my machines to get a rough idea of how stressed you are by using fingertip temperature. Next time you are getting ready to do something stressful—putting on your uniform for a contest of some kind, dressing for an important date, or waiting for the examination scores to be posted on the bulletin board—put your fingertips to your face and notice whether or not they feel cold. If they do, you can be sure your body is stressed and is undergoing some part of the fight-or-flight response. A little control of your breathing will help you to calm down again, if you want to calm down. If you are dressing for a contest, you will probably not want to be too calm. But certainly you want to be calm enough so that you can make good decisions once you get on the court or the field.

Another of my college students has had trouble making himself speak up when he is in a group. Any group at all. Classrooms, parties, hallways—whenever there are more than two or three people present he cannot make himself say anything. Of course, what has really been happening with this student (whom I shall call Bill) is that he has felt very stressed by other people. One of the effects of stress is to make it hard to think clearly and to take action based on clear thinking. Bill has been so stressed by other people that he cannot think clearly, and even when he does, he cannot take action (by speaking up) based on what he is thinking.

He, like Jane, now uses both breathing control and a different way of thinking about the problem to help himself relax in groups so that he can enjoy himself and speak up whenever he wants to say something. Bill is finding it hard work, and he still has a long way to go before he will feel satisfied, but he is already much better in groups than he can remember ever being before. One of the nicest things he and Jane and countless others have come to realize is that all of us *can* help ourselves do better in stressful situations if we just *will*. We are not at all helpless. We are not just "nervous people" who cannot do anything about it. We have *learned* to be nervous. That means we can *un*learn being nervous if we work at it.

Now I want to take you step-by-stressful-step through an imaginary situation, showing exactly how and when you might use breathing control to help yourself get through it. The situation I am going to imagine is one in which you are called upon to give an oral book report in English class. This means you will have to stand up in front of 30 of your friends and talk for five minutes about a book you have read and studied.

Let's say you are going to report on Mark Twain's *A Connecticut Yankee in King Arthur's Court*. You have read the book and found some of it funny, some of it boring, some of it interesting, and some of it confusing. You have decided that in your report you will first briefly describe what happens in the story, and then you will explain why you found it funny, boring, interesting, and confusing, mostly by giving examples from the book. Let's say you make some notes the night before and go to bed feeling sure that you have prepared satisfactorily but not at all sure that you will be able to give the report without making a fool of yourself by forgetting what you wanted to say, by stammering and stuttering, by trembling uncontrollably, by blushing with embarrassment, by having your voice quake and squeak, and so on.

Now is the time to begin using your breathing control as you lie there trying to get to sleep but worrying all the while about your report. Roll over on your stomach; proper breathing is easier when you are facing straight down. When we lie in other positions or stand or sit, we tend to use our chests to breathe, rather than our true breathing muscles down in the belly.

So lie with your chest on the bed and remind yourself that you really don't want your chest to be moving anyway. Then begin to think about your stomach muscles. Let them relax and think about how your stomach is gently and slowly pushing against the mattress as you breathe comfortably. As you relax and sense your breathing slowing down, begin to take two-second pauses between breaths. Each time your lungs empty, pause for a count of two before you take another breath. Don't force your breathing into a set pattern. Just relax and try to let this slow breathing begin to feel natural to you. Don't force. If the pause doesn't feel comfortable yet, be patient and continue your slow relaxed breathing. Imagine your heart becoming less and less stressed as you reduce your oxygen intake and allow your heart to beat slowly and comfortably. Don't worry about how you're doing; you're doing fine. Imagine the stress flowing out of your body as your slow, relaxed breathing continues into the night . . .

About twelve hours later you find yourself walking into your English class, nervously worrying again about how you're going to look and sound in front of the class. After the bell has rung and your classmates begin to settle down, work again on your breathing control. It is important that you get your heart rate down close to normal before time for you to begin your report. Breathe and pause. Breathe and pause. Relax. Think SLOW. You want everything in you to be going SLOW by the time you get up to speak. Heart rate, breathing rate, everything. You are going to move SLOW and speak SLOW and refuse to rush anything that you do during this class period. Concentrate on it. Slow everything down. Relax. You're in control. You're going to stay that way.

Finally the teacher asks you to go to the front of the class and give your oral report on *The Connecticut Yankee*. When your name is called, you do not jump up instantly, blush all over, and stumble hurriedly and miserably to the front. Instead, when your name is called, you calmly take one more slow breath while you gather your notes together, you slowly rise, looking over your notes calmly as you do, and you make your way to the front of the room at a comfortable, leisurely pace. When you arrive at the speaker's stand, you do not immediately begin to speak. You place your notes on the stand, continuing to look at them, and take still another slow breath. You concentrate on your breathing and on the opening sentence, not on the people sitting in front of you.

When you have taken a slow breath and arranged your notes properly, you think to yourself once more: GO SLOW. Then you begin to give your report carefully and clearly, looking up whenever you feel comfortable doing so. Occasionally you find yourself stammering or repeating words. When that happens, close your mouth for a second and remind yourself that you have been speeding up. It is almost impossible to stammer if you are relaxed, breathing properly with your heart rate near normal, and concentrating on the words in your notes. So when you make a mistake of any kind, close your mouth, pause, breathe correctly, and start once more. Continue to concentrate on your notes and not on what the teacher and your classmates are thinking of your performance. Relax, go slow, concentrate. The end of the report will come surprisingly soon. When it does, do not clutch frantically at your notes and race to your seat. Repeat your earlier pattern of taking another controlled breath while you gather your notes, then walk calmly to your seat, standing beside your seat momentarily rather than leaping into it. Then seat yourself, take another relaxing breath while you put your notes away, and then permit yourself to feel the glow of quiet satisfaction that we all feel after a job well done. You have been calm and poised, using your breathing control to stay in command of the situation. You deserve to feel good about yourself. Be proud. You were *good*.

CHAPTER V

Muscle Relaxation—Stress Control Technique #2

You will recall in Chapter IV that I suggested using breathing control to help yourself get to sleep the night before your oral report. I asked you to lie in bed with your stomach muscles completely relaxed as you began to reduce your breathing rate. Really, you were beginning even then to combine the first stress control technique, breathing control, with the second one, muscle relaxation. As we shall see in this chapter, these two techniques can go together very well in most stressful situations.

We have three kinds of muscle cells in our bodies—smooth muscle cells, cardiac muscle cells, and striated muscle cells. The first two kinds are found in muscles over which we exercise only a little direct control, such as those in the walls of the intestines or arteries. Or such as the heart itself. This extremely powerful muscle contracts as hard as it can about 40 million times a year for as long as you live. As with all of the smooth or cardiac muscles, it is harder to control your heart than your striated muscles. You can contract your bicep or your calf, both striated muscles, whenever you wish to. But smooth or cardiac muscles do not respond to your brain in that way. To make your heart muscle contract slower or faster, you must control something else—such as your breathing rate.

You can see why this is a good arrangement. Your heart muscle must contract more than 30,000 times every night in order to keep you alive until morning. If your heart had to wait until your brain ordered it to contract before it did so, you wouldn't last very long. Smooth and cardiac muscles continue to contract and relax—no matter what you are doing, no matter what you are thinking about, and no matter whether you are asleep or awake. You can and do make these muscles change their rate of contracting and relaxing, but only by talking first to something else in the body—such as your breathing—which will then "relay the message" to them.

You can see that in Chapter IV I was really talking about "smooth/cardiac muscle relaxation" even though I called the chapter "Breathing Control." You were learning breathing control in order to achieve smooth muscle relaxation. Now I want you to combine smooth/cardiac muscle relaxation with striated muscle relaxation. When you learn this, you will become an accomplished stress controller.

Most people's first thought is that it isn't hard to relax striated muscles. After all, if you want your arm to hang limply at your side, all you do is let it fall. Well, that's a good point. Unfortunately for us, however, the muscles in our arms don't have very much to do with stress. Think back. When was the last time you had an "arm ache" as the result of being uptight about getting your grade card for the semester?

The real question, of course, is when was the last time you had a headache, or a stomachache, or a backache, or a shoulder-neck ache? Most people do not have to think back too far to answer that question. Even if you are lucky enough not to have these kinds of aches often, that does not mean that you are good at relaxing your cranial (head) muscles, trapezius (neck and shoulder) muscles, upper and lower back muscles, pectoral (chest-shoulder) muscles, or abdominal (stomach) muscles. All of these striated muscle groups are heavily involved in your reactions to stressful events. Learning to relax them when you do not need them is an important step in becoming a skilled controller of stress.

Maybe you have never thought much about your cranial muscles. Maybe you never realized at all that your head is covered by muscles. You do know that you can wrinkle your forehead, though. And you know that some people can wiggle their ears. The incredible number of aspirin and other pain-relieving pills sold in the United States each year shows clearly that millions of Americans contract their cranial muscles any time they feel a little stressed. When you contract any muscle and keep it that way for a long time—say, a couple of hours—what happens? If you aren't sure, clench your fist tightly and keep it that way for only a couple of minutes. How does it feel? The result is *pain.*

Remember what I said in the last chapter about how people usually react to pain. They get more tense, which means that they contract those head or neck or stomach muscles even more, which means that their headache or stomachache gets even worse. Finally they take an aspirin and drug themselves into relaxing. Wouldn't it be nice for people to learn to control these muscles so that they wouldn't get the pain in the first place? And even if they did slip up and get a headache, wouldn't it be nice for them to be able just to relax some cranial muscles and get rid of it in a few seconds without pills? Well, no magic is needed—just a little determination and practice.

Technically speaking, the word "tension" refers only to muscles. A muscle can tense or relax—nothing else. Most of the striated muscles work in opposition to each other. For example, when you flex your bicep to bring your hand up to your shoulder, the bicep is tensing and the tricep, on the back of your arm, is relaxing. To straighten that arm you reverse the process. Most of you developed some bad habits when you were young. Probably just by watching other people react to stress, especially your parents and teachers, you may have begun to tense your forehead muscle (the frontalis) when you were working hard on some problem, or when you were getting angry, or whenever you began to feel stressed by something. The result? By now that frontalis muscle tension comes to you automatically, without your even thinking about it, whenever stress approaches. The result of that? Probably headaches from time to time.

Others of you developed different bad habits. Again from watching your parents and teachers react, you may have begun to tense the trapezius muscles in your upper shoulders and neck when you felt stressed. Watch the people around you for the next few days; notice that some of them carry their shoulders very high and forward, rather than having the chest out with shoulders back, low, and relaxed.

Often when I am seated with someone at lunch and he or she is talking about something that irritates, angers, or concerns him or her, I can see the shoulders start to creep up slowly. Trapezius tension.

Others of you have no doubt learned to tense your abdominal (stomach) muscles when you begin to feel stressed. It is hard to say how you learned that particular habit, since we usually cannot see someone else begin to tense the abdominal muscle group. Nevertheless, some of you surely learned to tense those muscles, too, and the result can be a severe stomachache. When people talk about stomachaches, you never know for sure what they mean, and they themselves may not know either. Some stomachaches are not muscular at all. They are the result of eating the wrong things, or they may be the result of worrying so much about something that the stomach begins to secrete its acids in such powerful composition that gases are formed, which become very painful. The long-term result of that secretion of too-powerful acids can be stomach ulcers, sores or even holes eaten into the stomach by the acids. Finally, some stomachaches are the result of both the worry-acid-gas combination and prolonged tension in the abdominal muscle group.

You can see that there is not necessarily any connection between stress and tension, since stress refers to a state of general nervousness and anxiety whereas tension refers only to tightening of the striated muscles. And yet those two words—stress and tension—have come to mean almost the same thing because most Americans have developed terrible muscle-tensing habits whenever they feel even a little stressed.

Are your upper and lower teeth touching each other right this second? I know that seems like a weird thing to ask, but your answer would tell me a lot about your tension levels if we were talking together right now. Do you see why? Well, unless you are munching on a snack, there is no reason for your upper and lower teeth to be touching. If they are touching, however, your jaw muscle must be tensed, right? Why is it tensed? Probably because you, like many people, have developed that bad habit even at your relatively young age. You have learned to carry tension around with you in that jaw muscle even when it has absolutely nothing to do.

Except when you are eating or talking, there should be a slight separation between upper and lower teeth. Keep your lips closed, relax your jaw muscle, and you will find that your lower teeth drop slightly away from the upper ones, right? Good. Work on that until you develop the habit of having a relaxed jaw muscle.

Why bother? Because you have to start somewhere. You cannot afford to keep the terrible habits that most Americans have learned of tensing muscles all over our bodies for no reason at all. The more stressed we become by our problems, the more muscles we tense and the more muscle power we put into each tense muscle.

The result of all this can eventually be tragic. Last year a woman in her late 50's came to me for help, having been referred to me by her doctors and one of her psychologists. It was disturbing to watch her move, because she was obviously in such great pain. She had learned the usual bad muscle tension habits when she was young, but as the years passed she had permitted her muscle tension to grow worse and worse in most of the striated muscles of her body, rather than in just one or two muscle groups. So, rather than suffering from severe headaches or frequent stomachaches, this woman suffered almost all the time from muscle tension pain throughout her body. Her arms hurt, her shoulders hurt, her head and neck were in pain, her lower back was in agony, and even her legs ached with tension. Her face was contorted with its own tension and with its reflection of the effort to withstand the pain elsewhere.

She talked to me about the pain of her life. She told me of the awful choice that she had faced for years—she could either take strong pain-killing drugs and deal with life in a groggy daze, or she could remain clear-headed but in unbearable pain. She talked of how impossible it had become for her to enjoy anything at all. Since virtually everything a person does requires the use of at least some striated muscles, she could no longer enjoy such simple things as eating (pain in jaw muscles and in arms and hands as she lifted her fork) or reading (pain in her hands as she tried to turn pages) or even watching television (pain in her back and neck as she held herself in a sitting position, even without movement).

As I began to try to help this woman, it became clear that the usual ways of helping people learn to control stress were not going to be effective with her. The things I have been writing about in this book had gotten beyond the reach of this woman. She could no longer command her muscles to do anything other than to grow more and more tensed.

Fortunately for her, however, stress control machines (biofeedback machines) have been developed that are capable of helping people even in such extreme cases. The electromyograph proved to be at least the start of an answer for this woman. With regular daily use of this machine, which signals to its user precisely how much tension is passing through any muscle group, she began to experience the first progress she had known in decades of ever-increasing tension. She began using the machine on her forearms, moving to other muscles only when she began to have at least slight relaxation in the forearms. Progress has been slow, but it continues.

Let me move to a person who is more "normal." Do you know Doug DeCinces? I don't know him personally either, but baseball fans certainly know his name and may have seen him play ball on television. He plays third base for the Baltimore Orioles. Early in the 1978 season, Doug's hitting was a disaster, at least by his standards. He felt he should have been hitting at a much higher average. About halfway through the season he got some advice from batting coaches, and that advice has apparently made all the difference. He finished the season as one of the best-hitting third basemen in baseball.

The advice? Just a little stress control. Specifically, he was advised to control his muscle tension when he went to the plate. Now, instead of standing and fidgeting all over the batter's box, instead of twitching the bat around in little jerks and circles while he awaits the next pitch, Doug just coils his body slightly, relaxes his muscles thoroughly, actually lets the bat rest comfort-

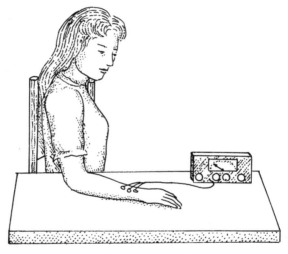

The electromyograph.

ably on his shoulder, and stands there—relaxed, alert, and ready to call on those untense muscles to snap into action if the pitch comes into his strike zone. As for the swing itself, he just concentrates on "throwing the bat" at the pitch (without letting it go, of course), rather than trying to out-muscle the ball. Doug has found that teaching his muscles to have less tension has made his job more enjoyable and has made him much better at doing his job as well.

Doug had a lot of company in the sort of nervous behavior he once showed. I'm not referring to baseball players; I'm talking about you and your friends. Watch them (and yourself) in class or at lunch or at a party. Look at those feet moving constantly under school desks—tapping the floor, tapping on the desk in front, swinging aimlessly back and forth. Notice your legs and feet as you eat your next meal. Are they in perpetual motion, or do you permit them to relax while you chew and swallow your food?

Does it matter? You bet it does! As I have said, you cannot afford to continue developing more and more bad habits. Learn to use whatever muscles you need in whatever you're doing— eating, writing, running, or talking—and let those other muscles relax. Remind yourself over and over until you finally begin to see some progress. Be determined to stay with it. A good distance runner and a good race horse are much alike in this regard. Their leg muscles are hard at work, but the other muscles in their bodies have practically no tension whatever.

Although I can't speak with authority about horses and their breathing control, I do know that good marathon runners are well aware of the need for control of their oxygen intake while running. Marathoners want their upper bodies to be very relaxed, with an absolute minimum of muscle tension in arms, neck, chest, and stomach; and they also want to be taking in the exact amount of oxygen needed to fuel their bodies comfortably for whatever pace they are running. They want their hearts beating at the lowest rate adequate to supply oxygenated blood to all parts of their bodies. So as they run they are combining the first and second stress control techniques I have described.

I said that breathing control (which leads to smooth/cardiac muscle control) and striated muscle control can fit together nicely. Let me describe now exactly how I combine these two techniques into a five-minute practice session that I make myself do every morning. *Every* morning. I try not to miss a single day. In order to remain "expert" at controlling my own stress, I have to practice. I practice five minutes a day. You may need less than that, or you may need more. That depends upon how stressed you think you are now and how *un*stressed you think it is important to become. Some of my students do not do any regular practice until their midsemester and then final examinations approach. Then they practice for five or ten minutes a day during the three weeks before and during those exams. You know yourself better than anyone else and can make your own decisions about your stress control practice.

My practice begins when my alarm clock goes off. My clock is electric and gives off a loud, irritating buzz that thoroughly destroys my sleep. But I like it that way. It gives me the first indication of whether I have been sleeping tense or relaxed. Many people are under the impression that they relax when they go to sleep. Not necessarily. Striated muscles are perfectly capable of retaining much, or even all, of their tension right through the night. So when my alarm buzzes at me, I can judge from my body's reaction whether or not I have been sleeping relaxed. If I have the "startle response"—a quick, uncontrolled contraction of the large striated muscles in the arms and legs— I know for sure that I have not spent a relaxed night. If the buzzer produces no startled contraction in those muscles, then I feel pleased that my muscles were not tensing during my sleep.

The next time you are with a group and there is a sudden, unexpected loud noise—a door slamming or a car backfiring —notice that some of the people will have the startle response and nearly jump out of their chairs, while others will not move at all except maybe for a blinking of the eyelids. The "jumpers" were tense; the "nonjumpers" had relaxed striated muscles.

So my alarm has done its thing and I am reluctantly awake and I know roughly how stressed I was during the night. I usually have a good feeling knowing that I won't be getting up—something I don't usually enjoy doing very much—for another five minutes. My entire practice session takes place right there in bed. Regardless of whether or not I slept tense according to my response to the alarm, the first thing I do is to go quickly through a short version of Jacobson's Progressive Relaxation Exercise. (A psychologist named Edmund Jacobson designed this exercise back in the 1930's.) You can try it now, as you are reading.

Start with your feet. Contract all the muscles in your toes, feet, and ankles so that they all scrunch together inside your shoes, if you're wearing shoes. Hold that contraction for a couple of seconds, then let all those muscles relax as completely as you can. Pause for several more seconds, thinking about the relaxation in your toes, feet, and ankles. Then contract your calf muscles. Hold the tension there for two seconds; then relax. Now put the tension into your thigh muscles (the quadriceps, on top of your thighs, and the hamstrings, underneath), hold that for another couple of seconds, and relax again. Pause and think about the feeling you now have throughout your legs, from the tops of your legs to the tips of your toes. Many people have learned such bad tension habits that they really don't know what a relaxed muscle feels like. Jacobson's Exercise can usually help, because one of the surest ways to get a striated muscle to relax is to tense it—*hard*—and then to release that tension.

To complete Jacobson's Exercise, simply repeat the tensing-relaxing pattern throughout the rest of your body. From your legs, move to your abdomen, then to your lower back, then to the pectoral muscles of the chest, then to your upper back and shoulders. Pause there for several more seconds to think about the relaxation you have now achieved throughout your legs and torso. Then, after repeating the tensing-relaxing pattern in your hands, forearms, and upper arms, move to your shoulders and on up to your neck, your jaw muscles, and, at last, your face.

Yes, of course you look dumb with your face scrunched up the way your feet were a couple of minutes ago. If you're reading this in class or in the library, I'll understand if you skip the facial tensing this time. But when you do the exercise alone at home don't fail to include those facial muscles. In fact, try to tense the muscles all over your head. Even though most people cannot feel anything happening when they first try to tense their cranial muscles (except maybe for a slight wiggling of the ears), get those muscles into this exercise right from the first—especially if you ever have tension headaches.

You have now gone through a brief version of Jacobson's Progressive Relaxation Exercise. If you have done it fairly well for your first time, you should feel somewhat more relaxed than you did several minutes ago. With daily practice, it can be a most effective way to get your large muscles to release most of their tension.

As I said, I lie in bed and zip through that exercise as soon as I have shut off the alarm clock. I do it now in about 30 seconds, which leaves me about four and a half minutes to complete my daily stress control practice session. Next, I count my pulse with my finger pressed into my neck, as I described in Chapter IV. Then I begin to think about my day. I start to picture some of the events and situations that I expect to happen before I return to bed seventeen hours from now. I imagine myself teaching the classes that are scheduled to meet, I imagine myself going to the library and getting assistance from the research librarians in finding some information I need, I picture myself going for my daily ten-mile run, I visualize myself at a meeting that may be scheduled. In other words, I select some of the upcoming activities of my day and try to imagine them in careful detail.

I force myself to imagine them going very badly for me. No, this is not the usual "hero daydream" that you and I engage in often. I do not picture myself going through the day making everything better for the world, saving the lives of beautiful women, and setting records in the marathon.

I lie there in bed imagining myself saying something controversial in class, for example, with the result that some of my students become angry and say nasty things to me. Or I may picture myself giving a speech about stress control and becoming very stressed during the presentation, stumbling over my words, forgetting the points I want to cover, and so on. Or I may imagine myself on a country road during my ten-mile run—running very fast because I am being chased by someone's unfriendly German shepherd.

Now, of the three things I just imagined, only the third one really has much of a chance to happen today. The other two are remotely possible but extremely unlikely.

That doesn't matter. The idea is not to try to guess exactly how your day will turn out and then to visualize your own prediction as it comes true. The idea is to picture some of the circumstances in which you will probably find yourself during the day and then to force yourself to picture these circumstances going badly for you.

To do this stress control practice correctly, you must take your daydream seriously. True, you are just playing a game. But the game has importance for you, and you must take it seriously for as long as it takes to play it.

The reason you are doing these things in your mind is so that, lying there in bed, you can practice the first two stress control techniques I have described. This is how I go about practicing them.

As I lie there imagining, let's say, someone becoming angry with me, I want to control my breathing and relax some of my important striated muscles, just as I would want to do if that situation really were to come up during the day. So, I picture Suzie the Student angrily talking to me about the low grade I have given her on her test paper, and I picture myself listening carefully to what she has to say. All the while, lying there in bed, I am taking two-second pauses between normal-sized breaths, and I am trying my best to keep complete relaxation in my stomach muscles, my neck-shoulder muscles, and my head-face-jaw muscles. As I continue to imagine this scene, I check on myself every half-minute or so. How is my breathing rate? Have I started to let myself breathe a little deeper or faster and has my heart rate begun to increase as a result? Is tension creeping into my jaw or my stomach? Am I able to listen to this imaginary angry person and yet remain unstressed by her anger?

I know that I need to practice this every day because several times a week I find that at some point in these few minutes of practice there *is* tension building up somewhere in my striated muscles or there *is* an increase in my breathing rate. After imagining this scene for two or three minutes, I complete the practice session by counting my pulse for a second time. Often I do find that it has increased somewhat during my imaginary stressful event. That is how I know that I need to continue my daily practice. I am not perfect at stress control. I never will be. But, with practice, I will be much better than I would otherwise be.

At the end of my practice session, if I find that my pulse has gone up, I usually lie still for another minute, continuing to control my breathing, continuing to relax, occasionally repeating Jacobson's Exercise as well, and just letting my mind relax, too.

Then, in my mind, I toss my practice session aside and forget about it until time to do it again tomorrow morning. It was a game I played so that I could practice these two stress control skills. IT WAS A GAME ONLY. I do not really expect my day to go badly. I never have. The German shepherd may be there, but I'll handle him. And I'll handle anything else that comes along, too. For the rest of my morning, then, I will be looking forward to whatever interesting and exciting things might come. If something stressful comes, I'm ready; but I'm not going to go around looking for it.

Any real unpleasantness that I may encounter will not necessarily, of course, turn out well just because I am using stress control techniques. But I know that if I handle my own stress well other people are usually able to handle theirs better, and we all have a good chance to get through the stresses of the day without disastrous results and with better solutions to problems and longer-lasting resolution of our conflicts.

I start my days with the kind of practice I have described. You may not want or need that kind of practice. That's fine. There are other types of stress control exercises such as Transcendental Meditation (TM) and Dr. Herbert Benson's Relaxation Response Exercise. These take longer than my type of practice session (about 20 minutes once or twice daily for both). If you are interested, you can find many books about TM, and Dr. Benson has written a book about his exercise entitled *The Relaxation Response.*

If you choose not to do any kind of daily practice, however,

I think you should at least give some thought to how you want to remind yourself to get relaxed striated muscles and relaxed smooth muscles when necessary. You may find that the techniques I describe in the next few chapters suit you better and help you achieve smooth and striated muscle relaxation as well. Or you may find that you need to come up with something totally different in order to achieve good muscle control. That's great. What I want is a YOU who is no more stressed than you really want to be—healthy, happy, enjoying your life, meeting its challenges. I am suggesting ideas that have helped me and many people with whom I have worked and whom I have taught. But we are all different from one another. Figure out what works for you, and do that.

To conclude this chapter, I want to tell you one of my favorite stories—one that I would like to think is true. It is about a brilliant university professor who was giving a magnificent lecture to several hundred students. As he lectured, pacing back and forth at the front of the auditorium, he held in his hand his notes, which consisted of a single 3 x 5-inch card. The professor roamed around the stage, making one complicated and insightful point after another. From time to time he would stop, close his mouth, study whatever was written on his tiny card, look up from the card, and then continue his lecture. He proceeded in this way for over an hour. At the conclusion, the students applauded in appreciation.

One of the students was brave enough to go to the front of the auditorium and ask the professor the question that had crossed the mind of every student in the class: "Sir, how could you possibly have gotten so much information onto one side of that tiny card that you could give such a terrific lecture for over an hour? What kind of system have you devised for making lecture notes for yourself?" The professor reached into his pocket and pulled out the card, showing it to the inquisitive student. Penciled at the center of the card was just one word: "Relax."

CHAPTER VI

How to Talk to Yourself—Stress Control Technique #3

This is the most important chapter in this book. I think you will see why as you read along.

Think back to Chapter V, in which I talked about stomachaches. You will recall that I said some stomachaches result from worrying so much about something that the stomach begins to secrete acids in such powerful composition that painful gases are formed. Think about what it means to "worry so much." When people say they worry, what they really mean is that they are talking to themselves about something stressful. They are talking to themselves in such a way that their bodies respond by ruining their own stomachs.

In Chapter IV I told about my student Jane, who became pregnant and was faced with the stress of having to tell her mother. I said that she decided to practice breathing control *and* to force herself to think about the problem differently. What she meant by thinking differently about the problem is exactly what I mean now about talking to yourself. There are good ways to talk to yourself and very poor ways.

All of us constantly talk to ourselves. What we say to ourselves really determines what kind of people we become. In fact, the whole question of how stressed you are depends on what you *say* to yourself about what is happening (or what just happened or what may happen soon). You have noticed, for example, that some of your friends do not get upset in the least about a thing that upsets you considerably. Why is that? Mainly because they are talking to themselves differently from the way you are. You may think of a plane trip as scary; they may think of a plane trip as exciting. Someone else may think of a plane flight as both scary and exciting.

The point is that the way we think of a particular thing is the result of how we have learned to talk to ourselves about that thing. Not that we necessarily go into a long speech to ourselves every time something comes up. Sometimes we do, but more often we automatically think of it in a certain way—it's scary, or it's exciting, or it's relaxing. What we usually don't notice is that this "automatic" thinking is not really automatic at all. It just seems so *because we have talked to ourselves in certain ways throughout most of our lives.* And that means, luckily, that we can change these "automatic" ways of thinking if we work on it.

Let me give you an example. In some of my classes I ask the students to submit a short paper every week. The paper is an informal description of some stressful event that occurred in the student's life during the previous week, followed by the student's analysis of why the event was so stressful and what he or she might have been able to do about it. When the students first begin to write these papers each semester, they are full of sentences such as: "She makes me so mad when she . . ." or "Exams get me so uptight . . ." or "Parties and dances make me so nervous . . ."

Whenever I read such a sentence I cross out part of it and change it to: *"I* make me so mad when I hear her say . . ." or *"I* make me so uptight when I take exams . . ." or *"I* make me so nervous when I go to parties and dances . . ." As the semester goes on, the students get better and better at mentally *taking responsibility* for their own anger, nervousness, and fear.

Nothing can make you mad except you. Nothing can make you uptight except you. Nothing can make you nervous except you. Nothing can make you stressed except you. You get mad if you talk to yourself in a certain way about what "she" said. You get uptight when you talk to yourself in a certain way about exams. You get nervous when you talk to yourself in a certain way about parties and dances. You get stressed because of what you say to you!

Other people and events and things do not stress you. *You* stress you. By taking a hard look at how you talk to yourself, and at different ways to do that very important thing, you will be looking at the very basic reasons for your having stress in the first place. Is it becoming clear why I said that this is the most important chapter in the book?

Think of five words or phrases that in your opinion describe you pretty well, words and phrases such as "nervous" or "tall" or "good dancer" or "clumsy" or "fast reader." Stop reading for a minute or two and think of five self-descriptions. If you have a pencil nearby, jot down the words or phrases that come to your mind.

Now think of five words or phrases that describe you as you would *like* to be if you could. Make these words and phrases correspond to your first list. For example, using my list, you might write "poised" and "tall" and "good dancer" and "well coordinated" and "fast reader." Take a look at your lists side by side. Are there important differences between the two?

Ask yourself how you feel about the differences. Is it at all stressful for you to think hard about the differences between what you think you are and what you would like to be? For most of us it is indeed stressful. Sometimes we can do something about our deficiencies and sometimes we cannot. A slow reader can read faster with instruction and practice. But if you are short and you want to be tall, there is not much you can do except wait to see whether you're going to grow any more. But you can always do something about the problem of being stressed by your deficiencies, and often learning not to be stressed by these deficiencies by talking differently to yourself will actually lead to changes in the way you *are*.

Do you find that hard to believe? Take this example, then. Suppose you are "shy" and you'd rather be "confident" and "outgoing." Think about the picture you have in your mind when you say to yourself, "I am shy," or "I am a shy person." Notice that you have the impression in your mind that shyness is a quality of your*self*. It seems to be a "thing" that somehow lives in your mind and body. Shyness is *in* there somewhere, isn't it?

No. It's not. We only talk that way to ourselves and to each other. But our language is misleading us. Shyness is not in there at all. For one thing, it is a mere word. Not a thing—a word! Think about that for a minute. Do you realize that we usually react to words as if they were something more than that? A word is just marks and squiggles on paper; or, if we speak it, it is just a noise. Squiggles and noises. That's all.

We have a squiggle-noise that we write this way: SHY. Look at that. Say that. Now explain to me how we can possibly come to think that this squiggle-noise is a quality that exists in our bodies. How do we manage to get so confused? Shyness is a *noise* we use *to describe the way we sometimes behave!* You can see, then, that we all "behave in ways we call shy" from time to time. Some of us "behave in ways we call shy" much of the time. But it always depends on the situation, doesn't it?

Of course it does. You may see yourself as an outgoing person, but there are times—around certain people or in certain situations you find a little uncomfortable—when you behave in ways we call shy. On the other hand, you may see yourself as a shy person, but there are times—around your family and closest friends or in some very comfortable situations—when you do *not* behave in ways we call shy.

I said a minute or two ago that not being stressed by the differences between what you "are" and what you'd like to be is something you can teach yourself by learning to talk to yourself differently. I said further that learning to be unstressed will often lead to actual changes in the way you *are*. Imagine, then, that you have always thought of yourself as a shy person. Imagine that you find this shyness a little stressful because you'd rather be a confident and outgoing person. Imagine that you begin to talk to yourself in a different way and on a regular basis, so that you are saying to yourself things like, "Well, I haven't spoken up in Social Studies class because I have been behaving in that class in ways we call shy." Or "I haven't asked Lisa to go to the movies with me because I have been behaving around her in ways we call shy." Wouldn't that make you feel a little different about yourself?

For most people whom I counsel and teach, making that change in the way they talk to themselves makes them feel considerably more relaxed about "being shy" (or whatever it is that they feel stressed about). They are able to realize that they have some *habits*—some ways of behaving that they have used over and over—and that these are merely behaviors, not qualities of themselves that *must* stay inside them. They feel less stressed because it's easier to think of having some habits that you'd rather not have than it is to think that you are a certain kind of person who must always be that certain kind of person because these "things" like shyness are inside you.

Once people finally begin to realize that they just have some behavior habits that they find somewhat stressful, and once they start talking to themselves differently about those habits so that they are less stressed about the habits, they often begin to find those habits slowly changing. After all, if you keep saying to yourself, "I haven't asked Lisa to go to the movies with me because I have been behaving around her in ways we call shy," not only will you feel more comfortable with yourself than if you keep condemning yourself for being a "shy person"—but also you will probably come to realize that just because you have behaved around *her* in a certain way does not mean you must behave around some other girl in that way. Or, that just because you behaved a certain way around Lisa yesterday does not necessarily mean that you must behave around her the same way tomorrow. Or, that just because you behaved a certain way around Lisa yesterday in regard to asking her to go to the movies does not necessarily mean that you must behave the same way in regard to asking her to go to the game with you.

Do you see what I'm getting at? Talking to yourself in sensible, less stressful ways will often lead you to relax your attitude toward yourself and toward some of your behaviors as well. You begin to realize that nobody behaves the same way all the time.

Even the bravest person you know does not always behave that way. Why? Because he or she does not have bravery sitting around inside himself or herself—"brave" is just a noise we use to describe the way he or she often acts. That person may not act that way tomorrow.

That's the way humans talk to themselves. Usually the wrong way. Try talking to yourself more sensibly. Don't let yourself label yourself. With those behaviors that you don't particularly like, talk to yourself correctly about them. They are behaviors that you have used in the past with certain people and in certain situations. That does not make you a "bad person," so don't be stressed by those behaviors. And since those behaviors were specific to you in the past and with some people and in certain situations, don't let yourself say to yourself that you must always behave that way in the future or with all people or in all situations. If you did talk that way to yourself, you wouldn't be telling yourself the truth. You would be stressing yourself considerably, and you would be keeping yourself from changing.

So shape up with this business of how you talk to yourself. It's vitally important to your happiness and your ability to succeed with whatever you'd like to do—make good grades, have good friends, do well athletically—that you learn to talk to yourself properly. Start now.

This is not, let me remind you, something that you should do instead of practicing breathing control (smooth/cardiac muscle control) and striated muscle control. Practicing those two skills should go hand in hand with practicing new ways to talk to yourself. In fact, the learning of any new skill usually entails changed self-talk as well. For example, learning to play a musical instrument is learning a new skill, but as you learn this skill your self-talk changes. If you play the guitar pretty well now, you can still remember a time when you did not. You can probably remember that as you developed the skill and strength to handle the instrument so that it made music instead of just noise, you also began to think of yourself as a "guitar player" and maybe as a "musician." You didn't purposely change your self-talk, but you naturally changed the way you talked to yourself as your guitar-playing skill developed. It should be the same with stress control, except that the changed self-talk should move away from self-labeling and should be done on purpose to help develop your breathing control and muscle relaxation skills.

There was a rather strange genius (or are they all strange?) who came to America from Europe early in the 1900's and who wrote a book called *Science and Sanity* (1933). In that book Alfred Korzybski makes a suggestion of an unusual and useful way in which we might talk to ourselves differently. He writes that using this technique in our minds will tend to help make us behave "more sanely." (His opinion is that most of us behave in "unsane" ways—not "insane" but not quite "sane" either—much of the time.)

Korzybski calls this technique "indexing and dating." No, not the sort of dating we have been talking about in this book. He means developing the mental habit of indexing and dating the nouns and pronouns that you read, that you hear other people speak, and that you yourself speak or say to yourself.

That sounds both confusing and impossible, but it's actually fairly simple and easy. Think, for example, of a school that for you is a rival, a school with which your school finds itself competing constantly in every way. How do you talk to yourself about that school? "Central High" does this or that? "They" do this or that? Korybski says to index and date "Central High" and "they." In your mind when you think of Central, you think "Central High (basketball coach/1976) is impossible to like." "Basketball coach" is the "index"; "1976" is the "date." It's not that there are 2,000 people at that school who are impossible to like. That's just the way we talk to ourselves about it. The fact is that Central's basketball coach seems impossible to like. But we're really talking about something he or she did several years ago (1976). There may be a new coach now, and even if there is not, that coach may have behaved in some awful way once or twice. Like you and me, that coach is not a "bad person"— that coach just behaves in certain ways at certain times.

Think of the number of times each day you hear someone talk about "they" or "them." What picture comes into your mind? "All" of some group of people? Is it really "all" of them that someone is referring to? What would happen if we developed the habit of indexing and dating as we talked to ourselves and other people?

Here is one sort of thing that might happen. When I was teaching at a university in the Rocky Mountain West, I had a group of students each fall many of whom were living away from home for the first time. They were mostly freshmen or transfer students; and most of the transfer students had gone to community colleges in their home towns for two years and only now had left home to complete their four years of college.

One of the assignments that I gave this group was to write a paper about some stressful event from the previous week and then analyze the event and his or her own actions. Each fall I found that I could expect the students' papers just after Thanksgiving vacation to be very unhappy. You would think otherwise, wouldn't you? These students had been away from home for three months, had returned for the first time, and had come back to college very unhappy.

Here's the way one of their late November papers might begin: "When I left home to come to college for the first time I was already looking forward to Thanksgiving vacation so that I could visit Mom and Dad, and my old high school, and my high school friends—and, of course, my boyfriend Bob who had been going steady with me for two years. But last week when vacation came, I found that everything had completely changed. I couldn't really talk with my parents, I visited the high school and nobody paid any attention to me at all, my friends didn't even seem like the same people I used to know so well, and even Bob seemed changed. I just don't know what happened!"

Each November so many of the students' papers sounded like that one that I began to return the papers just as the students had written them and to ask the class to rewrite the same papers for the following week—this time, however, with indexing and dating used throughout. The paper we just imagined would finally look like this: "When I (August) left home (August) to come to college (August) for the first time, I (August) was already looking forward to Thanksgiving vacation so that I (*November*) could visit Mom and Dad (*August!*), and my old high school (*June!!*), and my high school friends (*1968–72!!!*)—and, of course, my boyfriend Bob (August) . . . I (November) couldn't really talk with my parents (November), I (November) visited the high school (November) and nobody (Mrs. Jones, Coach Smith, Mr. Johnson) paid any attention to me (November) at all, my friends (Sally, Gwen, Rosa) didn't even seem like the same people (August) that I (August) used to know so well, and even Bob (November) seemed changed . . ."

You cannot imagine what a difference that rewriting usually made. The students would come back to class with their papers, smiling and shaking their heads that they had never realized that they had been talking to themselves in ways that made no sense at all. They found that they (November) could not possibly talk to a *memory* (August or June or 1968–1972). This little exercise in indexing and dating had made them see that they themselves had changed in three months. We tend not to notice that we change because we live with ourselves all the time. When we are away from other people for several months, the changes that occur in them seem large to us, since we were not around them from day to day and could not experience their very gradual changing.

Rewriting the paper also helped my students to see that it wasn't that "everything" was different or that "nobody" paid attention to them. In this case, it was Mrs. Jones, Coach Smith, and Mr. Johnson who were too busy to pay much attention when this graduated student visited her former high school. The fact that several other teachers, coaches, and students were indeed glad to see her simply escaped her notice because of the way she was talking to herself.

Think especially hard about the pronoun "I." We use that word to describe ourselves throughout our entire lives. We say things like "I did such and such when I was 10 years old," or "I'm going to do such and such before I'm 30 years old." But what is there about "I" (age 10) that is similar to "I" (age 30)? It's exactly the same word. But does it make any sense, really, to say that I am the "same person" 20 years later?

I, for example, am 38 years old as I write this. In 1950 I was 10 years old. Was that really "I" back in 1950? Are any of my 1950 ideas, values, and hopes still a part of me at my present age? Do I look the same? Do I think the same? Do I want the same things? Of course not.

The point is not that we should throw some of our words away. The point is that since we do not index and date in our heads as we think, talk, and listen or read, we often stress ourselves considerably by not realizing that we constantly change (and that we *should* constantly change), that other people do also, and that although we often say "they" or "all of them" or "Central High" or "nobody at all," what we really mean is "these certain, specific people." There is quite a difference. Changing your talking-to-yourself habits so that you automatically "translate" what others say to you (as well as what *you* say to you) can have an enormous impact on your stress levels.

Do you have the IFD disease? You probably do, at least at times, despite the fact that you have no fever and feel perfectly well. The IFD disease is a different kind of disease. Another genius—not quite so strange as Alfred Korzybski—named Wendell Johnson wrote about this disease in a book called *People in Quandaries.* Like Korzybski, he wasn't writing about stress control; he was writing because he, too, thought we would be "more sane" if we learned to talk to ourselves differently. I agree with them that we would be. I am also certain that we will be far less stressed if we index and date in our heads, as Korzybski suggested, and if we learn to handle this strange disease that Johnson wrote about.

IFD stands for "*Idealism,* which can lead to *Frustration,* which can lead to *Demoralization.*" The idea is not that we should not set high goals for ourselves. We should, of course, have high ideals. The point is that we talk to ourselves in ways that lead us to become frustrated and finally demoralized whenever we do not quite live up to our own ideals. Johnson says, "There is no failure in nature." He means that when you "fail" to do something, it is you who decides that you have failed. There is no absolute standard that insists that you have failed.

For example, suppose you try to make straight A's on each report card you get at school. You try for an A in every single course, every grading period. Well, that's great. Set your ideals high. But talk to yourself "sanely" too. Realize that the straight-A report card is *your* idea (or your parents' idea, or somebody's idea), but that not making straight A's means "failure" only if you accept that idea for yourself. If you get a report with five A's and a B, you can call yourself a failure if you like. But you are not! "Failure," remember, is a noise or, if written, some squiggles on paper. Since you are much more than a noise or some squiggles, you cannot be a failure.

What has happened is that you have *behaved* in such a way that *you have earned a reward that fails to equal the reward you wanted.* That's too bad. But don't give yourself the IFD disease because of it. Don't let yourself become Frustrated and then Demoralized because of it. Relax. You did your best. Ask yourself if you want to keep the same goals for the next grading period. If you do, then keep those goals and give it another shot. But, above all, talk to yourself correctly about this. If you do, you will avoid IFD disease, you will be less stressed, and you will have a much better chance of studying well and succeeding with your goals than if you get yourself tied up in a mental knot about your previous "failure" and your fear of another "failure."

One of my graduate students has often had a bad case of IFD disease. She has always expected herself to do everything to perfection, no matter what it was. Cleaning house, making A's in school, knitting a sweater—she had to be perfect every time. One of the results of her unsane self-talk was frequent, crushingly painful migraine headaches. Maybe you yourself have migraines. Probably you at least know someone who does. If so, then you know that a migraine usually wipes a person totally out for at least a full day and often longer than that, and nothing really helps. There is just tremendous pain so that the person feels only like lying down and crying—except that crying seems to make the pain even worse.

This particular student tried virtually every stress control approach that I knew, plus some that she dreamed up herself. What finally has worked for her has been a different way of talking to herself about the things she tries to do. She has gone through a long, tough process of learning to keep her goals high without making them unreasonably, impossibly high. Does every weed have to be pulled out of her garden? Or just enough so that her vegetables can be healthy? She is learning to arrange the goals in her life so that she can *try* to be "perfect" about the truly important things. But she is teaching herself, too, that real perfection is a goal that we human beings will usually not quite reach, and that this is okay. The idea is to make the very best efforts we can, with our stress under control so that we *can* make our best efforts, and then to talk to ourselves correctly about our results. Did we make it? Great! Let's control our stress that well on the next try so that we'll be able to do it again. Did we miss it? Okay. That doesn't make us "failures." That means we behaved in such a way that we did not achieve at the level we ourselves had decided we wanted to. Now, instead of getting the IFD disease, we will sit down and make decisions about what we ought to try next.

Many of you are probably not fully aware of the power of your own self-talk. The class for high school juniors that I have been teaching for several years on Saturday mornings has seldom been fully aware of this until it completes my "pain test." Remember in Chapter II I told you about that class and the rappeling exercise I arrange for the students to do each semester? Their pain test is a wall-sit exercise that I have them do twice, once early in the semester and again near the end.

In the first test, the 15 boys and 15 girls (3 from each of 10 area high schools) line up with their backs against one wall of the gymnasium. On my signal to begin, all 30 students bend their knees to a 90-degree angle so that they are sitting with their backs pressed against the wall and nothing supporting their

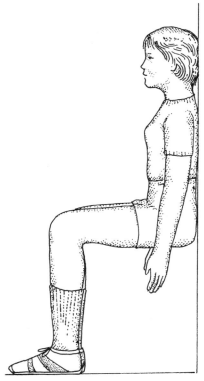

The pain test.

bodies except the strength of their quadricep muscles (the large muscles on the top of the thigh). If you have never tried this, stop reading for a moment and do it for just a few seconds. I want you to know what it feels like.

If you tried it, you can tell that this will become very painful in just a short while, depending upon such things as the strength of your quadricep muscles, the weight of your upper body, and so on. Under the circumstances I described, all 30 students immediately begin to compete with each other. No one wants to sink to the floor first. No one wants to be second. Everyone hopes to beat the two people on each side of himself or herself. The boys want to beat the girls. The girls want to beat the boys. The Canton High students want to beat the Potsdam High students. The Potsdam High students want to beat the Canton High students.

Last spring, the first student to give in and sink to the floor did so after 1 minute 15 seconds. The champion for that day stayed up for exactly 4 minutes. All the students seemed pretty sure that they had stayed up as long as they possibly could. The average time for the 30 students was 2 minutes 20 seconds.

As the semester goes on, I work with that group on how to talk to yourself when participating in athletic contests (this course deals with sports and stress control, as you may remember). We work on psyching up when we need to do that and on psyching down when we ought to do that. We practice stress control, and we practice talking to ourselves so as to get just the right amount of muscle power or relaxation to do our athletic jobs really well.

At no time do the students ever practice the pain test.

Near the semester's end, I have the students repeat the wall-sit, but under very different circumstances. This time, I make it impossible for them to compete with each other. I arrange things in another part of the athletic building so that none of the students can see each other while they are doing the pain test. They have no idea how they are doing compared to each other. They are not even told how much time is passing, so that they cannot know whether or not they are beating their previous times.

What I do ask them to do is to talk to themselves so that they are not thinking at all about the pain in their quadriceps or about the time as it drags by. I simply ask that they control their self-talk for as long as they can and relax the muscles that are not in use. You can see, then, that they are really using the second and third stress control techniques discussed in this book—muscle relaxation and self-talk control.

The results are always amazing to the students, and sometimes even to me. Last spring only one student failed to improve on his first performance, even though many of the students expected to do less well than the first time because they would not be able to compete against each other. The champion on this second test was a girl, who improved from 3 minutes on the first wall-sit to 8 minutes 15 seconds on the second. The average time for all students on the second test was 4 minutes 36 seconds. The class average improved, then, from 2:20 to 4:36, an almost exact doubling of its original performance.

As I said before, I suspect many of you are probably not fully aware of the power of your own self-talk. Your power is actually enormous. You can exert unbelievable control upon your stress levels if you practice talking to yourself in the ways I have suggested in this chapter. You really are in charge of your life and the way you live it. Make your choices about what and how you want to be, then talk to yourself in ways that will get you there. Your mind is a super-powerful instrument that can take you and your body almost anywhere you'd like to go. Just give it a chance.

One type of stress problem that I have not discussed yet is the situation in which you find yourself worrying about something that happened yesterday or last week or last year—and you cannot stop being stressed by the memory of it. All of us from time to time will do something stupid or klutzy or embarrassing. You may not feel particularly stressed at the time this occurs—you may even laugh your way through the embarrassment. But later, recalling the event, you begin to feel considerable stress. "Why did I have to say that?" you ask yourself repeatedly. And the memory stays and stays . . .

Breathing control and muscle relaxation are very useful in this kind of situation. But so can self-talk be. Try talking to yourself in ways that are "descriptive" rather than "judgmental." Judgmental self-talk usually involves labeling yourself or your actions with words that put some value on what happened—words like bad, clumsy, awkward, dumb, foolish. Descriptive self-talk, on the other hand, involves the use of words that simply portray the event as a movie camera might, without putting a value judgment on it.

A good example of this from sports occurs frequently on the

university's women's basketball team that my wife coaches. During free-throw practice, often she or I will observe one of the women beginning to have a problem (such as missing several consecutively or seven out of ten) and to get upset (clenching her fists, shaking her head, and so on). If my wife or I walk up to the shooter and ask how she is talking to herself after each shot, we usually hear something like, "*Another* bad one," or "That's three misses in a row. What's *wrong?*" or "I can't believe I am doing so poorly."

We then remind the shooter to use descriptive rather than judgmental self-talk. With this reminder, we leave her to work out the problem herself. What she will then do after a missed shot is to say things to herself like, "That was off to the left," or "That was several inches too short." The difference in the way she will *feel* about each miss is crucial. Instead of being increasingly stressed by her errors—and thereby putting more and more tension into her muscles, and consequently missing more and more as she continues—she simply describes what happened. Short. Long. Left. Right. Flat. No backspin.

Not only is she not stressing herself by the way she is talking to herself, but she is even telling herself something useful that should help with the next shot. If the shots are falling a little short and she talks to herself about that, she ought to be able to get a little more arch and distance on the coming attempts.

As for the embarrassing thing you may have said yesterday at the lunch table, change the way you have been talking to yourself about that. Instead of wallowing in the embarrassment in your mind, just let yourself recall the event (if you *must* recall it at all) the way a movie camera would, resolve to handle that kind of situation some other way next time, apologize to somebody if you think you ought to, and get on with the business of living your life. And by the way, a good apology goes beautifully with breathing control and muscle relaxation. It can even become a very pleasant experience.

There is something I had better explain before we go any further. You may be getting the impression, as others occasionally do when I teach or give a talk on the subject of stress control techniques, that I'm saying that a good stress controller never shows any "negative" emotion at all. He or she will show "positive" ones such as joy, love, excitement, happiness, but never anger or fear or frustration or sadness or disappointment.

I am certainly in favor of showing positive emotions, but I am not always against showing negative ones, too. Suppose, for example, that something tragic happens in your life. Let's say that a pet dog that has been with your family since you were a young child is hit by a truck and killed. If you loved that animal, you are going to be very stressed by his death. Well, you *should* cry! Even if you are a boy, you should cry. We males are usually taught early in our lives that only sissies cry, and that's too bad, because when we are stressed by sadness like this, crying will help our minds and bodies handle the stress of the sadness. In fact, holding the tears back will only lead to increased stress— the very opposite of what we want.

But what about anger? Am I saying that we all should throw temper tantrums when we get furious? Not exactly. If you talk to yourself correctly so that you are (1) taking responsibility for events ("I make me mad"); (2) thinking of your behavior rather than labeling yourself ("I sometimes behave in ways we call shy"); (3) indexing and dating in your mind; (4) avoiding the IFD disease; and (5) using description rather than judgment in your self-talk—you will find that you are getting furious much less often than you did before. I can almost guarantee that.

But when you do get angry, do not "bottle it up." If you really have allowed yourself to get furious, you must express that fury somehow for the sake of your own stress levels. Think about what is happening inside you. Remember the discussion in Chapter IV about the "fight-or-flight response"—those automatic things your body begins to do when it thinks you are going to want it to engage in some strenuous exercise (such as fighting for your life or running for your life)?

If you have let yourself become furious about something, the fight-or-flight response is going off inside you. At that point, the only smart thing to do from a stress standpoint is to give the fight-or-flight response something physical to do with itself. For example, the tremendously powerful natural hormone adrenalin will be released into your bloodstream by your adrenal glands. If you give yourself nothing physical to do, this hormone will make you feel as if you are going to explode right on the spot, and in a sense you will.

This does not mean that you must physically attack whomever you are angry at. That's often a good way to get into a lot more trouble than you need. It does mean that if you possibly can without dire consequences you should express your anger as clearly and straightforwardly and with as much maturity as you can ("I am *so* angry with you for doing such and such to so and so"), and then you should take a long walk or get on your bike and ride for ten minutes or go to the gym for a workout. I realize that you can't always do one of those things. You may have a class, or a meeting, or some other thing that will prevent your taking the right action for your stress levels. In those situations it becomes especially vital to utilize the stress control skills that you do have: control your breathing, relax your striated muscles, talk to yourself correctly and with determination that you are not going to destroy your own insides just because of someone else's behavior.

The healthiest people are usually vigorous people who have learned good stress control skills and who seldom get extremely upset or angry. But when they do get upset or angry, they know very well that they must express their thoughts and feelings as clearly as they can and then "work it off" physically as soon as they can arrange to do so.

I hope I have been able to make this clear to you. It is an important point, since none of us is going to become such a perfect stress controller as never again to lose his or her temper. When that does happen, we need to know what to do about it. In Chapter IX an idea is presented which, if you decide to use the technique, can be of great help if you find yourself unable to "work off your steam" after something stressful.

In concluding this chapter, I would like to emphasize again the tremendous importance of working on the ways in which you talk to yourself. I suspect that many of you—maybe most of you, maybe nearly all of you—are like me at your age. By that I mean that you are doing a lot of the things you do because of fear. Are you surprised that I knew? Most of the people who come to me for counseling are fearful—that is why they are so stressed. But what they don't realize is that nearly everyone is fearful.

As I think back to when I was a high school student myself, I realize that most of the things I did were done because I was afraid not to. Most of the things I did not do were avoided because I was afraid to try. Most of you are the same way. I don't mean that people look at you and know you are afraid. Most people think that only they themselves are afraid. I was regarded as a fairly tough guy—a pretty good athlete—in high school and college. But it was only when I learned how to talk to myself that I finally began to relax and do things just because they seemed like good things to do and not because I was afraid not to. I realized at that point the truth of what I have written at the start of this chapter. I realized that the whole question of how stressed you are depends on what you say to yourself about what is happening, and that this really determines what sort of person you become.

Since I was in my late 20's when I began to talk to myself differently, and began really to enjoy life more than I ever had, and began to look forward to each day because I no longer had persistent fears, I remember thinking that I wished someone had made it clear to me ten years earlier that there were different ways I could have talked to myself about my life. That's why I'm writing this book for you, and not for your parents. I care about them, too, but I don't want you to ruin these great years of your youth being stressed by life and afraid to take charge of your own. As one of my favorite coaches used to say to us: "You've got to get *yourself* ready to play this game. Ain't nobody gonna do it for you!"

CHAPTER VII

Counting Down—Stress Control Technique #4

I wish you could somehow get to know my very good friends "Gunner" and "Fritz" (Dr. Hugh Gunnison and Dr. Theodore Renick). These two psychologists have during the past few years devised and perfected an effective stress control technique that they call Fantasy Relaxation. I have decided not to try to present their entire technique in this book, but I do think you should become familiar with one important part of it —the part they call Counting Down. I have changed their Countdown procedure a little, but the credit for the technique is theirs entirely. I want you to be able to use Counting Down partly because it is such an effective technique itself and partly because it can so easily serve as your "trigger"—your cue or mental reminder—to get yourself quickly into any or all of the first three stress control techniques that I have presented so far.

As with the other techniques, Counting Down ought to be practiced in private in order to be most useful when you encounter stressful situations, but, also like the others, you can simply start using this technique without any practice at all. You yourself will have to answer the question of how skilled you want to be with the technique.

In Chapter II when I first mentioned my Saturday morning high school class on stress and athletics, I mentioned the rappeling session we hold during which the students try to relax while hanging 40 feet above the ground. I said that, since rappeling requires almost no muscular effort, each student tries to be completely psyched down in order to do this mountain-descending technique well and to enjoy it too. I added that by using a few stress control ideas most of these students have been able to maintain their usual heart rates and normal stress levels even under these frightening circumstances.

Counting Down has proved to be the most popular technique during the rappeling session. The majority of successful rappelers (those who managed to have normal stress levels throughout the descent) used Counting Down as their trigger to get themselves quickly into breathing control, muscle relaxation, and self-talk-control.

These same students also tended to prefer Counting Down when on another Saturday morning I took them to the indoor swimming pool and invited them to jump off the high diving board while blindfolded. Again, this was a situation in which little muscle power was needed, and thus very low stress levels were appropriate—just a lot of mental concentration so as to keep themselves precisely upright while dropping 12 feet into the water without the benefit of sight. Most of the successful jumpers stood on the end of the board, Counted Down, and then stepped off into space.

By now you are probably becoming impatient to know what it was that Gunner and Fritz dreamed up in the first place. Be patient just a minute more. I'm giving you a little practice in controlling your stress! Relax while I say one other thing before getting into a discussion of Counting Down.

I need to assure you that when you actually use the technique in a stressful situation no one else will know you are using it. You will be doing something *inside yourself,* as with the first three techniques, to control your reaction to a stressor. I like to say that before starting to describe Counting Down, because this *practice* procedure *is* something that other people would notice if they were watching you try it. But the *practice* is to be done when you're alone, not with spectators around.

If you are reading this alone in your room, you can practice Counting Down for the first time as you read along. But it's going to be fairly hard work, so be ready to use some energy.

If you happen to be lying down, move to a chair or stand up. I'll be able to explain better if your head is "up" and your feet

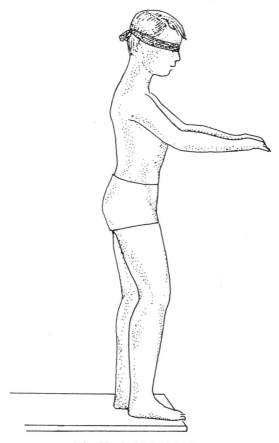

The blindfolded high dive.

are "down." If you are lying down, portions of the explanation may be unclear.

Mentally divide your body into three parts. In your mind draw one dividing line just under your shoulders and another at hip level. Part Three, above the first line, will be your head, shoulders, and arms. Part Two, between the two imaginary lines, will be your torso—chest, stomach, upper and lower back, and internal organs. Part One, below the second imaginary line, will be your legs and feet.

Here is the way you practice. Again, remember that this is not

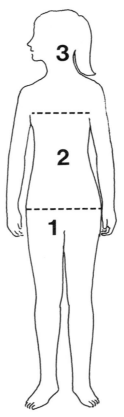

The countdown sections.

exactly how you will use the technique in front of other people. Start with Part Three. As soon as you feel ready, put maximum tension in all your striated muscles in Part Three. Hold that tension for at least 20 seconds. Your cranial muscles and the muscles in your face, jaw, neck, upper shoulders, upper and lower arms, and fists should be squeezed and straining as hard as they can while the rest of your body tries to remain relaxed. Try to keep your breathing as normal as possible. Your breathing rate will, of course, increase gradually as you go through the practice, because your large muscles are working very hard and will demand the circulation of more oxygenated blood from the heart.

At the end of about 20 seconds of Part Three tension, say to yourself "Three" and at that instant relax those straining muscles and let your mind focus on that good, sweet feeling of tired relaxation. Try to remember exactly how those muscles feel at that relaxed moment. Really focus on it. Be focused mentally and relaxed physically.

After 15 or 20 seconds of relaxation, you are ready for Part Two. Contract as hard as you can the striated muscles in your chest, abdomen, and back. Again, hold the tension for about 20 seconds. Then say to yourself sharply "Two" and let all those muscles go limp. Now focus your mind on those relaxed muscles. Remember the feeling.

Finally, after another 15 or 20 seconds of relaxation, tense those huge, long muscles in your thighs, calves, and feet. Hang onto the tension for 20 more long seconds before you finally allow yourself to say "One" in your mind so that you can let the tension go. Relax Part One and think about the feeling of relaxation you now have throughout your legs. After about 15 seconds of focusing entirely on your legs' relaxation, let your focus broaden so that you are thinking about the muscle relaxation throughout your whole body. It's a good feeling, isn't it?

Now go through the whole process again, but this time make it a little faster. Hold each tension section for just 10 seconds, and focus on the relaxed muscles for only 5 seconds before going on to the next one. Then relax for a full minute, thinking about your overall sense of relaxation.

Hang in there. There is more to come. Now tense your entire body and release the tension in each part as you Count Down. Count "Three . . . Two . . . One . . ." with no pause between the sections at all. After each series of Three-Two-One, relax for a minute or so and think about how the tension has dropped down through your body so that it finally, as Gunner or Fritz might say, "lies in a little pool at your feet!"

Practice until you feel tired. That's enough for your first

practice session. I recommend that you practice that way several times weekly until you feel you can use this technique skillfully in stressful situations. But let me explain quickly how you are going to use it in public. When you encounter some stressor, simply repeat "Three-Two-One" to yourself as quickly or slowly as you need to. With each mental count, let yourself remember the relaxation you experienced in practice at the end of each tension period.

What you are doing with your practice is building up a kind of "muscle memory." That may sound odd, but—because your nervous system branches out all over your body—your muscles do indeed have a kind of memory. In fact, it is exactly that muscle memory that you are developing when you do a basketball lay-up thousands and thousands of times until you no longer have to think about what is truly a very complicated muscular skill. Or when you play guitar chords thousands and thousands of times until you no longer have to stop and talk to yourself in order to get your fingers on the correct strings.

Your Counting Down practice is designed to build up your muscle memory of exactly how it feels in each of the three parts of your body to be completely relaxed. The time you spend at the end of each Countdown focusing on how your body feels with that "pool of tension" down at your feet is the key to your successful practice of Counting Down. You are teaching your muscles that when you say to yourself "Three-Two-One" they are to return to that untense state that they should remember from your practice sessions.

Use Counting Down as frequently as you like—from one to 100 times or more daily—so that you can do the actual counting in a split second of time without really having to go through much of a thought process at all and without having to take your mind off of whatever you are doing. In most stressful situations, after all, we do not have time mentally to "check out" for several seconds. We often have to react immediately to the stressor; we very frequently have to "think fast" in order to handle the problem well.

Let me say again that when you use Counting Down to handle stressors, you do *not* tense your muscles. The actual tensing of muscles is only part of the practice sessions. At school, at work, at the job interview, at the dance—your Countdown is to activate the muscle memory of the extremely relaxed muscles that you have focused upon during practice, not of the tensed muscles that preceded the relaxation. Obviously, then, your Countdown will not be visible to other people if you do it properly.

Let's look now at a good beginner's example—one that does not require you to talk your way through the stressful situation. Picture yourself at the dentist's office. You know you will not have to give a speech or argue with someone or defend yourself in any way. But you also know from experience that this may be a tough situation from a stress standpoint, and you know that the best way to handle what could be a painful experience is to relax as much as you can.

Imagine yourself, then, reading a magazine at the dentist's office. You are relaxed, controlling your breathing, and talking to yourself sanely about this appointment. ("*I* make me nervous in the dentist's chair . . . Pain is partly dependent upon my reaction to the dental drill . . . A relaxed body will feel far less pain than a tensed one . . . I will behave in ways that will reduce the pain; my previous tension in the dentist's chair does not have to affect my behavior today . . . I am in charge of my own behavior—no one else can be . . .")

Your name is called by the receptionist. You feel a wave of alarm and anxiety racing through your body. The fight-or-flight response! "Three . . . Two . . . One . . ." As you put your magazine away you feel the relaxation and calmness returning as your muscle memory undercuts your fight-or-flight response. The pounding in your chest subsides as your heart rate returns gradually to normal, and you walk toward the dentist's chair.

What has happened is that your Countdown has served not only to relax your muscles but also as a trigger to remind you, almost without your conscious attention to your breathing rate, to cut your oxygen intake. Your smooth/cardiac muscles have gradually responded to this signal, as we saw in Chapter V.

You seat yourself and begin to stare at the familiar apparatus in front of you. Your eyes move to the small dental tools on the shelf beside you and then up to the drill itself. You feel your stomach tightening and your jaw muscle tensing as you recall painful experiences and anticipate today's pain. "Three . . . Two . . . One . . ." Relaxation returns to your striated muscles, and again you find that your Countdown has led you to untense your jaw and stomach and also has triggered your mind to return to its sane self-talk.

Once the dentist begins to work and you realize that drilling is indeed going to be necessary again, you are going to need all your stress control techniques at once. Count yourself Down once more to relieve your striated tension and make sure that your jaw muscles will be relaxed throughout the drilling. Maintain consistent two-second pauses in breathing to get the smooth muscle control you'll need. And remember the pain test. Remember that those high school students doubled their wall-sit times (and, in a sense, reduced their pain by half) by talking to themselves correctly. They took their minds completely away from the quadricep tension and felt comparatively little pain; you must do the same here *by taking your mind somewhere else.* If you have practiced, you will undoubtedly be so effective that you can leave the dentist's office with an overwhelming sense of accomplishment. Even without practice, you can almost certainly experience less pain than you have had in previous drillings.

You can see, then, how these techniques should go together to obtain the greatest possible stress control. I strongly recommend that you develop the habit of using the Countdown as your trigger. It has proven to be a reliable way to get directly into muscle relaxation and to snap your mind into the breathing control and self-talk-control that are so crucial in really tough stress control situations.

Some people try a stress control technique without truly believing that it will have any effect. Sometimes that kind of doubt prevents a technique's working very well, but often a technique works despite a person's skeptical attitude toward it. While

teaching a college course in stress control, one morning I intro-
duced the students to Counting Down. We practiced the Countdown several times in class and discussed its use as a trigger to
get into other techniques.

A few minutes after the class had ended, one of my students
came to my office excitedly to tell me what she had just done.
She had gone across the street to the Registrar's Office to pick
up her grade card for the past semester. She had been terrified,
because she feared that she had made D's in two of her courses.
She didn't really want to pick up the card at all, but she knew
she would have to get the news sometime, and she wanted to do
it then so she could stop wondering and doubting and worrying
about those two grades.

She told me that when she walked up to the Registrar's desk
her heart was pounding so hard that she felt she had to lean
against the counter in order to remain on her feet. And she said
that, even though she felt silly doing it and didn't expect it to
work, she Counted Down. She stood and waited for several
minutes as the Registrar looked up her grade card. You can
imagine her surprise when she realized that she actually was
beginning to feel more calm. By the time her card was handed
to her, she felt almost entirely normal and was able to accept the
card, look at it, see that one of the grades was indeed a D (while
the other one she had feared so much was a B), and walk out
of that office with her stress quite under control.

She told me that she did, of course, feel disappointed at the
D but at the same time felt amazed and proud that she had
handled that scary situation without "coming unglued," as she
put it. And she had been so excited that she had run back across
the street to tell me about her triumph.

I wanted to tell you that story to emphasize the fact that
these techniques can work even if you do not practice and do
not really expect them to work. But imagine how much more
effective you could be with practice and with the confidence
in your ability to use the techniques that would come as a result
of practice.

Some of you are athletes. Even if you are not interested in

athletics, though, you may be interested in Counting *Up* occasionally. In working with athletes and with the high school stress and athletics course, I have found that there are times—especially in playing some sports—when reversing Gunner and Fritz's Counting Down procedure can be useful. To practice Counting Up, first do the usual Countdown practice. After completing the exercise and after the final minute of focusing mentally upon your overall relaxation, say to yourself sharply "One." At that instant, put tension back into Part One. (Notice that you are reversing the usual order of counting.) Almost immediately, say to yourself "Two" and add Part Two tension to that which you already hold in Part One. Again immediately, add Part Three so that you have cranked tension into your whole body.

Always practice Counting Up much more rapidly than you practice Counting Down. You want your body to learn that the rapid "One-Two-Three" sequence is its cue to psych up. In actual use, the Countdown can be done just as quickly as the Countup (in less than a second if necessary). By keeping this slight difference in the speed of your Countdown and Countup practice, however, you will enable your mind and body to continue to react to the "Three," the "Two," and the "One" as relaxation cues, but to a rapid "One-Two-Three" as a cue to psych up quickly.

Combine your Counting Up with an increase in your breathing rate and with appropriate self-talk. ("I *can* psych myself up to play defense . . . I *won't* feel tired until this game ends . . . I *will* dive for that ball on the floor . . .") Stress control, as you see, means putting your stress level wherever you need it to be at the moment; it does not always mean reducing your stress level. For most of us, most of the time, we do not need any help in getting ourselves "up." In fact, we are usually too good at that. But there are occasions when this Counting Up skill may prove helpful.

In Chapter II I mentioned that I visited a high school class each Friday for six weeks, talking about stress control for taking examinations. Even though I taught the students for only 15 minutes each visit, their exam scores came up measurably.

The two techniques that I chose to teach them during this very short period of instruction (only 90 minutes altogether) were breathing control and Counting Down. Since many students tend to feel panic when they receive an exam paper or when they come to specific questions that they can't answer right away, breathing control and Counting Down can clearly be helpful in fighting this kind of stress. Self-talk-control can be the most helpful of all in preparing for examinations, but there was not enough time for me to teach so complex a technique to this particular class.

There is no doubt that we can all think more clearly when we control our stress levels. It is not yet completely clear why our minds function so much better when we are only a little psyched up, but my research and that of many others consistently shows that this is true. It may be that some of the hormones we begin to release during the fight-or-flight response have a brief retarding effect in many areas of the brain. There is already some evidence that this happens, but you need not wait until we researchers are sure how everything happens. You should be getting on with learning to get your stress levels where you want them so that you can live a full, happy life and succeed in doing whatever you choose to do.

I was interrupted while writing that last paragraph by a phone call from a university student who is not in any of my classes. She said that she is preparing to enter medical school when she graduates next year, but that she is finding herself unable to handle her stress. Premedical courses are extremely demanding—chemistry, physics, biology, biochemistry, psychology—and students feel that they must always make A's in order to have a good chance to be accepted into medical school.

I will be meeting with her tomorrow to see what I can do to help her. What will I suggest? I will probably ask her to begin immediately with the Physical Conditioning Procedure that I shall describe for you in Chapter IX. Then I will start to work with her on breathing control, muscle relaxation, self-talk-control, and finally, Counting Down. At age 20 she is already in serious trouble, with stomach and intestinal upsets and tension headaches. I hope you won't wait that long. Even if you are only 15 years old as you read this, start putting this book to good use right now. It is *not* okay to wait five more years.

CHAPTER VIII

Positive Mental Rehearsal—Stress Control Technique #5

Most of you do an interesting thing to yourselves as the time to do something stressful draws near. You worry about it—that is, you imagine how this stressful thing may turn out and you picture yourself being yelled at or "freezing" in front of an audience or "drawing a blank" with a test paper in front of you or saying incredibly dumb things on the telephone to fill up the silences after you've asked someone for a date.

The interesting thing is that you are giving your brain (and its branching nervous system) a tremendous amount of practice. Practice at what? At doing exactly what you hope it won't do when the stressful event comes.

In other words, your usual way of thinking about upcoming happenings that you fear may turn out to be unhappy or scary or infuriating or frustrating makes it much more likely that those happenings *will* turn out badly. (And even if they don't, think of the energy you have wasted while making yourself miserable.) Worrying about what is coming, then, not only is wasteful and useless, but it also tends to make us do a lot worse than we otherwise would have done.

Obviously, one very smart way to "worry" is to use the kind of "sane" self-talk that we discussed in Chapter VI. Talking to yourself about your behaviors (instead of self-labeling), indexing and dating, short-circuiting the IFD disease, taking complete responsibility in your self-talk for whatever will occur, being descriptive rather than judgmental—all these new mental habits will greatly reduce the stress you feel as this potentially stressful thing approaches. It is also likely that you will *do* better when it

71

comes if you change the ways in which you have talked to yourself in the past.

You may talk to yourself quite correctly, however, and still be not only stressing yourself but also "practicing" doing the worst possible things because of what you're picturing in your mind. So I am talking now not only about the words you speak inside your brain but about the pictures you create there, as well.

Suppose at school you receive a note directing you to report to the principal's office tomorrow morning before classes begin. After you have Counted Down, gotten into your other techniques so that you have shut off the fight-or-flight response, and begun some sensible self-talk—what do you picture in your mind? Or suppose you have a visit scheduled to the campus of a college you may want to enter next year, and you have arranged an appointment with the Admissions Director—what do you picture in your mind? Or suppose you are planning to telephone someone tonight to invite her or him to go to a homecoming dance—again, what are you going to picture in your mind?

If you picture your typical "worrying" scenes—you and the principal becoming very angry with each other, or your sitting nervous and stupidly "blank" while the Admissions Director tosses questions at you about why you think you want to enroll in that particular college, or your voice trembling nervously while you recite some little planned speech (don't tell me you've written it down!) on the telephone—you are stressing yourself and *rehearsing the wrong behaviors.*

Controlling the pictures in your mind is a difficult feat. Most people need months of self-discipline before they can do it consistently, and probably no one ever gets the kind of sure control that you are perhaps already developing over your striated muscle tension. Frankly, it's not very important or even necessarily desirable that you get the same kind of control of your mental pictures.

But when you do have something stressful scheduled to happen tonight or tomorrow or next weekend or next month, you should set aside five minutes a day (or five minutes every other day if the event is still months away) during which you give your brain and nervous system some good, strong practice in doing this thing right. It's hard to do anything well without some correct practice. When we talk about mental-picture-practice for stress control and for improved future behavior, we are talking about what I call Positive Mental Rehearsal.

Let me give you an example. About six years ago the time was getting near for the birth of someone who turned out to be our youngest daughter, Julie. For the first time, I was invited by the doctor to be in the delivery room with my wife when she gave birth. You would think that I would have been delighted, wouldn't you? Well, I was and yet I wasn't.

I very much wanted to be there for the birth, and I talked to myself correctly about that. But the *picture* in my mind was a stressful one for me. As I imagined myself watching childbirth, I found myself feeling queasy in the stomach; I found my striated muscles beginning to tighten, especially in my abdomen; I felt my pulse quicken and my breathing rate increase. In short, I found myself so stressed by the *pictures* in my head that I wasn't sure I wanted to tell the doctor that I would be there.

At that time I had not yet developed the techniques of breathing control and muscle relaxation, and I had never met Fritz and Gunner and so knew nothing about Counting Down. I did know how to do correct self-talk, but I was still bothered by the pictures that I saw in my mind when I imagined myself in the delivery room with the doctor.

At that point I tried my first serious stress control experiment with myself. I decided to set aside five minutes each day during which I would find a place to be alone and utilize the Positive Mental Rehearsal idea.

The technique I developed had two parts. It seemed to me that it should work, based upon what I knew about the brain and the nervous system. For the first two or three minutes of my Rehearsal, I would picture the delivery room as if I were looking into it through a small window. I would picture myself standing beside the operating table, I would picture my wife lying on the table ready for the childbirth, and I would picture the doctor and her medical helpers in their gowns and operating-room masks along with the equipment that is part of an operating or delivery room. That leads me to an important point. In order to do Positive Mental Rehearsal well, you should have the clearest, most accurate picture in your mind that you can get. That may mean visiting a particular scene or room in advance of your scheduled visit, or looking up someone's photograph in a yearbook or newspaper, or finding pictures of something in an encyclopedia—anything that will help your mental pictures to be as accurate as possible.

In my case I knew, of course, what the doctor looked like and what my wife looked like, and I could picture an operating or delivery room clearly from film scenes and television dramas. I could also picture childbirth with some accuracy, since I had watched films that showed at least portions of the delivery of a baby.

I also knew what I myself looked like. Remember that in the first part of Positive Mental Rehearsal, you are picturing looking at yourself as well as the other people involved. So I could easily spend the first two or three minutes of my Rehearsal viewing this scene from my imaginary window in the delivery room. I pictured my wife working hard to help the baby out and the doctor helping the process with her hands—and, very importantly, I pictured myself standing beside my wife and the doctor. I forced my mental picture of me to be a "Positive" one. I saw myself standing there, looking straight at the parts of childbirth that were difficult for me to want to view—the episiotomy, the afterbirth, the small amounts of blood and other fluids—and I pictured myself calm, strong, helpful, happy, excited, and finally overjoyed at what I was seeing. The birth of our baby!

This picture was not an easy one for me to force upon my mind at first. It was hard for me to picture myself as excited and overjoyed at the same time that I pictured myself looking at those parts of childbirth that I was interpreting in stressful ways.

But I did it. And I worked at it. As the days went by, I became much better at seeing both things at once—an excited and happy and relaxed "me" looking at what I had always viewed as stressful.

The second part of Positive Mental Rehearsal was a little more difficult. For the final two or three minutes of the Rehearsal I switched my picture of the delivery room scene so that I was no longer looking at me and the others from the outside. I moved myself mentally so that I was now inside of my own head, looking down at my wife and at the impending childbirth, standing next to the delivery table and to the doctor and her assistants. I found it harder to feel excited, happy, and relaxed while picturing this scene from inside my own head than while picturing myself from the outside. But I worked hard, forcing myself to look at the stressful portions of the delivery and imagining at the same time that I was unstressed (remember that I had not yet developed the breathing control and muscle relaxation techniques).

During my first eight or ten Rehearsals, in fact, I felt that I was making no progress at all toward feeling the way I wanted to during the second part of my Rehearsal. But I had only a few more weeks before the baby was due to arrive, and so I simply became more determined. Finally it began to work. I found that if, during the first part of the Rehearsal, I began to concentrate very hard on my picture of myself—this relaxed, calm, enthusiastic person standing beside the doctor—and then made the switch from part one to part two with a determined, almost angry, swiftness, I could at last begin to feel a lessening of my stress levels as I got into my own imaginary head.

As the final two weeks passed and I continued my Positive Mental Rehearsal for five minutes each day, I improved steadily until, during the last three or four Rehearsals, I could make the mental switch from part one to part two with confidence that I could be just as excited and relaxed from inside my own mind as I had taught myself to be from my imagined position outside the delivery room.

You will be surprised to learn, perhaps, that I still did not have confidence that I was actually going to be able to do this thing when the real-life situation arose. I developed confidence in my ability to do the Positive Mental Rehearsal well, but I was then just beginning to create and utilize this technique, and even though I knew enough about the brain and the nervous system to be pretty sure that it would work—how could I be really sure? Since I had doubts whether or not the technique would work in the actual stressful situation, wouldn't those doubts make it even less likely that I would be successful?

The fact that I had so many doubts about this and yet it still worked perfectly was a real shock to me. I stood there in the delivery room fully expecting to be highly stressed—queasy stomach, tense abdomen, high pulse and breathing rates—and was amazed to find that I was not. I actually felt just what I had Rehearsed. Still more surprising to me, I felt no sense at all of "fighting down" these stressful feelings. I felt perfectly natural standing there, very much as the doctor herself seemed to be— enthusiastic-yet-calm, strong-yet-tender, relaxed-yet-overjoyed. I look back now at that event as one of the high points, one of the most meaningful experiences of my life. It was the Positive Mental Rehearsal that enabled me to have that fantastic experience and to enjoy every minute of it despite my doubts that the technique would work.

This technique will be even more successful for you because you understand breathing control and muscle relaxation. The portion of Positive Mental Rehearsal that for me was so difficult, that shift from the first to the second part, will no doubt be much easier for you since you can shift from outside to inside your own head while using breathing control and muscle relaxation (and using those techniques later when you actually go through the stressful situation, of course).

Another of my graduate students, a 30-year-old man, recently did something that most adults find extraordinarily stressful— he quit his job. And not just a job, but a career that had looked very promising to him for most of his life. We have already imagined job interviews or college entrance interviews as examples of stressful situations that you may face soon. But think how much more stressful his situation must have seemed to him. He had a family to support and felt he needed not only a new job but a new career—immediately!

As the time drew near for Don (not his real name) to fly to Philadelphia for a crucial interview, he began to practice Positive Mental Rehearsal as we had worked on it in my stress control course. Don read everything he could find about how to handle an interview well—how to dress, how to shake hands, how to sit, how to handle questions, and so forth. Then he put these things into his Rehearsals so that his brain and nervous system (don't forget that you're Rehearsing your "muscle memory" too) would have daily practice in behaving correctly at the actual interview.

Don flew to Philadelphia the day before his scheduled appointment to avoid feeling the stress and anxiety that a tight schedule usually brings. He did not want to have to worry about rushing from one plane to another, hurrying to a taxi, racing against time in order not to be late for his interview, or forgetting some of his materials in his haste. He traveled in a relaxed frame of mind, occasionally practicing his Positive Mental Rehearsal during the day, knowing that a missed connection would be no disaster.

After checking into his hotel, he took a relaxed walk to the building at which he was to have his interview the following morning. He looked at the building and at the floor on which his interview would take place, imagining as best he could what the interior of the offices might look like. Then he went to a movie that he thought might be funny and entertaining, got a good night's sleep (using the sleep-inviting breathing control technique I described in Chapter IV), and got up early so that again he would not be rushed in getting to his appointment on time.

As he dressed, ate breakfast, gathered his materials, walked once more to the interview place, and sat in the waiting room reading a magazine, Don used all the stress control techniques we have talked about so far. But once he was called into the interviewer's office, he didn't need to think of his techniques at all. Why? Because he had already practiced the interview a hundred times. His Positive Mental Rehearsals had prepared him to be relaxed, calm, poised, and assertive but polite. Don said he felt he was going through his tenth interview, rather than his first. He not only handled himself exactly as he wanted to, but he was able actually to enjoy the hour-long experience rather than feeling tense and miserable throughout.

An important part of Don's Positive Mental Rehearsals, a part that you probably should include in yours, was picturing himself doing the other techniques skillfully, too. He Rehearsed breathing control and muscle relaxation, for example. That is why he didn't need to think of his techniques at all during the interview. He had pictured himself doing them so much that they came automatically. He found, too, as do most people, that Rehearsing the technique of self-talk-control made the interview more enjoyable. It is important, for example, to talk to yourself in that situation about the fact that you want to ask some questions, too. That means that you have some control in the situation; you are not at the mercy of someone else. You need to talk to yourself about your own needs for information about the job. You want to know its drawbacks as well as its good points. This is what I meant when I said that Don Rehearsed being assertive but polite. He wanted to interview the interviewer. (Most interviewers think more highly of you if you do ask some tough questions in a polite way.)

Sooner or later in your life, your ability to handle the stress of an interview is almost certain to be crucial for you. Positive Mental Rehearsal that includes the Rehearsal of all your other techniques is the surest way both to do well in the interview and to enjoy it as well. I want you to know about one extreme interview procedure so that your own Positive Mental Rehearsals about interviews can include the toughest situation you might ever face. The roughest interviewer I have ever known is a man who until recently was an administrator in a large city school district. Every spring he interviewed hundreds of young people, hoping to find a few dozen who would be good enough to work for him. These interviewees were a little older than you probably are, having in most cases just graduated from college, but for many of them this was one of the first job interviews they had had.

The administrator, whom I shall call Dr. Smith, would ask the candidate to sit down and then in a friendly fashion would say, "Well, why don't you tell me about yourself?" The candidate might talk for a few minutes about where he or she was born, might say something about high school and college backgrounds, and might comment on hopes and plans for the future.

Dr. Smith, no longer smiling now, would then ask again, "Well, why don't you tell me about yourself?" Usually the candidate would pause in some confusion, wonder what to say next, and then try to talk about himself or herself in different terms, such as educational philosophy or educational psychology.

Dr. Smith, now scowling in anger, would lean across his desk and, contempt and disgust dripping from his voice, would carefully say to the candidate: "I am a very busy man. I do not have time to sit here and listen to this garbage you continue to speak at me. I have a hundred candidates who want this job that you seem determined to throw out the window. Now, for the last time, TELL ME ABOUT YOURSELF!"

Have you been imagining yourself in that situation as you read? How do you think you would react to that kind of treatment? Would you feel crushed? Furious? Why do you think Dr. Smith was behaving that way? What do you think he was hoping to find?

Well, he told me he was hoping to find a few dozen young people each spring who could handle the stress that he was trying to create in them. He wanted to hire people who could take that kind of pressure without falling apart. His idea was that, if someone went to work under him, he or she was eventually going to be confronted with a student or parent or teacher or administrator who was just as hateful and unreasonable as he, Dr. Smith, was trying to be in the interview.

Ideally, Dr. Smith wanted to find young people who, when they heard him say for the third time, "Tell me about yourself!"

would look him squarely in the eye, maybe smile briefly, and tell him in an assertive but polite voice, "Dr. Smith, if you want me to tell you about myself you are going to have to treat me a little differently. You are going to have to tell me exactly what kinds of things you want me to talk about, because I can't read your mind. You are going to have to treat me like a human being as well, because whether you realize it or not, that's exactly what I am." And then, still looking Dr. Smith in the eye, the candidate might (Dr. Smith hoped) sit back, relax, smile, and wait for his reply to *that*.

As I said, I wanted you to know about Dr. Smith's interviewing style because your Positive Mental Rehearsals ought to include some of the toughest situations you can picture. If the real situation turns out to be not nearly so tough, that's fine; but you will have been prepared for anything. That means that your Positive Mental Rehearsals should include picturing yourself using the other stress control techniques—especially self-talk-control. Tell yourself the truth about your stressful situations, which is that you always have some control over what happens. You can always inform someone firmly and politely that you are a person with rights of your own, and that you insist on being treated that way. You *always, always* have control over your own insides. And that is the truth!

You will recall the five-minute "Worry Exercise" that I do every morning (which I described in Chapter V), in which I try to picture the events coming up in my day and imagine those events going badly. I don't want you to think that the Worry Exercise has the same purpose as Positive Mental Rehearsal. They are both stress control techniques, but they are not used for the same reasons.

In the Worry Exercise I do not try to look at myself and the other people involved in my day through an imaginary window in a room. That means, of course, that I do not do the first stage of Positive Mental Rehearsal. But the Worry Exercise *is* similar to the second stage of the Rehearsal. I do look through my own eyes at something that I am imagining to be stressful for me. The difference lies in the fact that in the Exercise I simply picture the stressor and try to do my breathing control and muscle relaxation well. I don't go any further than that; I don't picture myself being poised and calm nor replying "sanely" to the person who is angry with me, nor do I work on self-talk-control.

In other words, the Worry Exercise has more limited use than does Positive Mental Rehearsal. It simply allows me to practice two stress control techniques on a daily basis. I use Positive Mental Rehearsal for the major stressors scheduled to come up in my life, not for the daily events. For example, if I have a speech or address to make to a large audience, I may use Positive Mental Rehearsal for several days before and probably use it several more times on the day of the address. In the Rehearsal I will be Rehearsing everything—breathing control, muscle re-laxation, self-talk-control, and possibly Counting Down for use during my walk to the speaker's stand; eventually I will Rehearse the beginning sentences of the address itself. But I do begin every day with the Worry Exercise, regardless of whatever else I may do to practice stress control during that day.

One of the most important things you should be developing as you approach the time when people will think of you as an "adult" (another of those labels that people use in their self-talk) is what we call "self-confidence." Be careful how you talk to yourself about that, too. Do you say things like, "He has self-confidence" or "I don't have self-confidence"? Notice that the way you just said that leads you to think that self-confidence is some*thing* that exists inside you—or does not exist inside you. Remember from Chapter VI the correct way to talk to yourself about these things—"He sometimes behaves in ways that we call self-confident" or "I sometimes have behaved in ways that we do not call self-confident."

If you do not think of yourself as a self-confident person—which really means only that you have labeled yourself because, like most of us, you sometimes feel stressed, nervous, and tense in certain situations—you should use Positive Mental Rehearsal regularly. It will enable you to practice new habits and behaviors that will allow others to begin to think of you differently and, more importantly, will allow *you* to begin to think of you differently.

In other words, what we call self-confidence can be nothing more than a decision you make that you will utilize Positive Mental Rehearsal regularly enough so that your behaviors begin slowly to change. Rehearsal is, in one sense, nothing more than mental practice in self-confident behavior so that your real behaviors will also have a chance to develop in that direction. The people you know who seem to you supremely self-confident are—if they think and behave that way inside themselves as well as outside—not stressed, tense, and miserable when they are "under pressure." They have taught themselves to enjoy pressure. They know that they can handle their own stress levels well, and so they are free to find pressure situations interesting.

Doesn't that make sense, after all? If the only thing you can truly enjoy in life is sitting in your room or watching television, because then you feel no pressure and no stress, I'm afraid you are going to miss the *living* of life almost entirely. Life can be a fascinating, exciting, rewarding experience if you get out there in the middle of it. Use the kinds of mental practice we have talked about in this book. You may find your*self* beginning to follow your mind into the middle of all those "stressors" out there, beginning to think of those stressors as more interesting than stressful, and, finally, beginning to look forward to living each day. Remember, you can teach yourself to become whatever you decide that you prefer to be. Decide soon.

CHAPTER IX

Physical Conditioning Procedure—Stress Control Technique #6

Nearly everybody (unfortunately) thinks he or she already knows all there is to know about exercise. In fact, almost none of you, I'm afraid, understands physical conditioning very well.

If you're like most people, young or old, you think that you condition your body by playing sports, by working hard at lawn chores or shoveling snow, or just by being very busy and active. None of those activities is likely to give you the kind of conditioning I am going to suggest that you do for stress control.

In Chapter VI I discussed expressing your anger rather than "bottling it up inside." I said that anger will set your fight-or-flight response in motion, and that if you're furious and give yourself nothing physical to do, the adrenalin and other hormones released into your bloodstream will drive up your pulse and blood pressure, pump tension into your whole body, make it difficult to think clearly—in general make you feel like a "stress bomb" ready to explode. I said that correct self-talk-control will lead you to lose your temper far less often (and so help you not to make a fool of yourself very often, too), but that once you have angered yourself, your body will demand action.

I explained further that, although you can and usually should express your anger (with as much maturity as you can), you should follow up by taking a walk or a bike ride or by having a gym workout. Finally, I said that I knew you couldn't always arrange to do those things because of your busy schedule, and I promised that in Chapter IX I would give you a technique to help with this problem that we all face regularly.

Well, this is Chapter IX. I have already insulted you by saying that you probably don't understand physical conditioning. The reason you must come to understand it is that if you devote an hour a week to the Physical Conditioning Procedure described in this chapter, your failures in stress control are unlikely to have damaging effects on your body. None of you, after all, is going to use self-talk-control perfectly every minute of every day. None of you, after all, will become so good at breathing control, muscle relaxation, Counting Down, and Positive Mental Rehearsal that you will never stress yourself again. This Conditioning Procedure, if you do it correctly, will make it possible for you to go ahead and be an imperfect stress controller (as I am!) and still have a reasonably healthy, unstressed body and usually a clearer-thinking, less troubled mind.

I said earlier that most people think you condition your body by playing sports, by working hard around the house, or by being very busy and active. I won't say it's impossible to condition yourself for stress control by doing those things. I'll just say that it would be very rare.

To put it simply, being very busy and active does not usually involve anything strenuous. You hustle from one class to the next, you type half the night writing a report for science class, you jump in your car and hurry to an evening meeting of some kind—and it's easy not to notice that you're still spending almost the entire day sitting down at a desk, or at the lunch table, or in a car.

Working hard around the house usually fools us, too. Sometimes the work is strenuous, like shoveling snow. But it is seldom sustained (carried out for, say, 20 minutes without pausing) and almost never is it regular (say, every other day for weeks and months on end).

Sports fool us most of all. No sport in itself gives us a sure-fire stress control effect. Many sports are too strenuous to be useful for stress control conditioning—wrestling, for example, or basketball, or lacrosse. Other sports are not strenuous enough, such as golf, or bowling, or even baseball and softball. A few sports might work, depending upon how you and your team play them. Soccer and field hockey might do, for example.

Almost anything, including sports, can be fairly unstressful and so may not hurt you from a stress control standpoint—*if* you have a certain attitude toward it. If you thoroughly enjoy the activity, look forward to it, and can handle your own lack of success with it (such as being second-string on a team or losing three games in a row), it's probably not stressing you much. But almost certainly it will not provide the stress control conditioning that I am going to suggest.

I am not going to ask you to drop your sports or change them to soccer or field hockey or anything like that. I'm going to suggest that you find an additional hour a week to undertake this Physical Conditioning Procedure stress control technique that will allow you to be less than perfect with your other stress control techniques and yet will keep you healthy and probably thinking more clearly now and throughout your life if you continue the technique into adulthood. Many people nearly fall out of their chairs when they hear that. "Another *hour* per week? You're kidding! I don't have another *minute* to spare in my week!"

Well, it's your life, my friend.

If you "don't have another minute to spare" you're probably the person who needs this technique the most. Grim statistics show that your super-busy life may turn out to be somewhat shorter than it would have been had you learned to take better care of yourself. Like everything else in stress control, however, only you can decide whether or not using a particular technique is worth the attention it will require.

Before I go on, let me remind you of something you already know. See a doctor before you start. Don't assume that simply because this Physical Conditioning Procedure is less strenuous than wrestling or basketball or lacrosse you can't possibly hurt yourself by jumping into it right away. You can always get in trouble if you ask your heart to do something it is not ready to do. Explain to your doctor what you are planning to do and get his or her okay. Then start.

The Committee on Exercise of the American Heart Association has for years studied the minimum exercise levels required to condition our bodies. The Committee finds that we humans can condition our bodies by doing a certain minimum amount of work weekly. What I want you to do for stress control conditioning is near that minimum, but I have some changes to suggest in the AHA's procedure, and I also insist on a certain *mental* approach to the Physical Conditioning Procedure. Do this in addition to (or instead of) whatever "exercise" you now do. It will take 20 minutes a day, three times a week on alternate days (Monday, Wednesday, Friday, for example, or Tuesday, Thursday, Saturday). If you do it for much longer than that, you are no longer doing it just for stress control. Do this exact procedure. Any less will not be enough to achieve the conditioning effect. Any more can become stressful.

The idea is to get your heart going at 70 percent (or a little less) of its maximum rate for those full 20 minutes, three times weekly. No more than 70 percent; maybe a little less, but not much. Get your pulse to 70 percent and keep it there for the full 20 minutes. I'll tell you in a minute how you can figure out what heart rate that would be for you, but first I'll tell you what exercise this will probably include.

Three kinds of activities fit in very well with this Physical Conditioning Procedure. One of them is the walk-jog-run activity. (If you live in snow country, then walk-jog-run on cross-country skis.) I use the three words "walk-jog-run," of course, because the question of which one you will do depends on your own 70 percent pulse rate. If you find that your pulse rate needs to be 150 beats per minute in order to hit 70 percent of your maximum, you will probably have to go at a gentle run. If your pulse rate needs to be 135 beats per minute, a slow jog may do it for you. At your age, I doubt that walking will make it for most of you, but it might. (With older people such as your grandparents a brisk walk is usually all that is required; as you will see, your age becomes part of the arithmetic to find your 70 percent figure.)

The second kind of activity that fits well into a Physical Conditioning Procedure for stress control is swimming, and the third is bicycle riding. You may settle on one of these three, or you may decide to use them alternately. Just about any activity other than those three would have to be changed too much in order to fit the heart-rate requirement. If you like tennis, for example, and want that to be your Physical Conditioning Procedure, think what you will have to do to make it work. You will have to run at about half speed to get to the ball, because if you sprint around the court your heart rate will go much higher than 70 percent of its maximum during each point. Then between points, while you're picking up the tennis balls or waiting for your opponent to get ready, your heart rate will drop far below the 70 percent figure, and that will not work.

You must get your pulse to 70 percent of maximum and keep if there or just slightly below that figure for 20 consecutive minutes, three times a week. Any more than that will be stressful; any less will not achieve the conditioning effect. It will not do to play tennis (or anything else) for five hours hoping that your heart will hit the 70 percent rate enough in the five hours to add up to 20 minutes. This constant stressing then unstressing will not provide your body with what it needs for stress control conditioning.

If this sounds terrible for some reason—too much work, too much time, too boring, or whatever—all I can say is "Give it a chance." Probably you have never tried anything like this. Most athletes, in particular, find it very difficult at first to do it correctly. They are accustomed to going as hard as they can for as long as they can while training for their sport. That is the way to train for your sport, of course. But the purpose of this is stress control conditioning. This is a gentle procedure. Very, very gentle, compared with preparing to compete on the wrestling mat, on the lacrosse field, or on the basketball court.

On the other hand, it is strenuous compared with sitting in your car or at the supper table or strolling down the halls at school or taking notes in class. For those of you who are accustomed to doing almost nothing physically for much of the day and then expending the huge amounts of energy that, say, basketball practice demands, this Physical Conditioning Procedure will be very difficult at first. It is an "in-between" kind of activity. But if you try it for several weeks or months and continue to hate it, you should probably quit.

Your mental approach is important, just as it is in all areas of stress control. Hating something, no matter what it is, is stressful. Hatred may, in fact, be the most stressful state of mind of all. If you try this Physical Conditioning Procedure—really give it a fair chance—and continue to find yourself dreading it, you should not continue to do it. You will have to become so good at the other stress control techniques that you keep your stress levels where you want them without the benefit of the Conditioning Procedure. Most people learn to love the Conditioning Procedure. Most people, once they become confident that they are doing it correctly, look forward to the 20-minute activity because they find it delightful (whether they do it with a friend or alone), because it takes them away from their stressors for a while, because they find themselves thinking more clearly about their problems, or just because they never feel quite so "alive" as when they're doing it.

You're impatient to know the arithmetic formula for finding your 70 percent. Okay, here's what you do. Find your normal, resting pulse rate. Do this while you are seated, and do it on more than one day to make sure you have your normal rate. If you take it only once and you happened to be going through a stressful day, your reading will be higher than normal. (If you have forgotten how to take your pulse, see Chapter IV.)

If your normal pulse rate is between 70 and 80 beats per minute, you are average. That doesn't mean you are good or bad—it merely means that you have the same pulse, roughly, as do most other people. The first number you will use in figuring your target pulse rate is 220. But use that number only if your normal resting pulse was 70–80. If your pulse was not in that range, add to or subtract from 220 the number of beats you were below 70 or above 80.

Here are two examples. If your resting pulse was 55, your resting pulse is 15 beats per minute below the bottom of the average range (70–80). Subtract 15 from 220 and use 205 as your first number in the arithmetic formula. If your resting rate was 90, your resting pulse is 10 beats per minute above the top of the average range (70–80). Add 10 to 220 and use 230 as your first number in the arithmetic formula.

Let us call your first number "220-modified" to show that you start with 220 or with your own modification of (addition to or subtraction from) that figure, depending upon your resting pulse. Here is the formula:

220-modified, minus your age, multiplied by .70.

Here is an example. Suppose a 16-year-old named Karen takes her resting pulse each morning for several days and finds that her pulse is 65 the first morning, 67 the next, and 63 the next. She decides to use 65 as her normal rate. Since that is five beats per minute lower than the 70–80 average, she subtracts five from 220. So her "220-modified" is 215. The next step in the formula calls for her to subtract her age from "220-modified." She subtracts 16 from 215 and gets 199. That is her approximate maximum heart rate. Finally, she takes 70 percent of that figure by multiplying 199 times .70. This result, 139, is her target pulse rate for her Physical Conditioning Procedure. Karen will try to get her pulse to 139 or just below that for 20 consecutive minutes, three times a week, by jog-running, by swimming, or by bike riding. If she does, she can be the sort of imperfect stress controller that we are all sure to be and still be likely to remain very healthy and perhaps to think more clearly about her problems and stressors, too. In making these calculations, there is no difference in the formula for males and females.

My students always want to know how they can possibly

figure out their pulse while they are running. Good question. Go back to Karen's target of 139 and imagine that she is walking out of her house to experiment with different speeds of jog-running as she searches for the speed that will get her pulse into the 140 neighborhood. She knows her resting pulse—65 beats per minute. To find her walking-speed pulse, she will walk at her usual pace for a minute or two. Then, looking at her watch (which must have a second hand on it), she will come to a quick stop and immediately press her finger to her throat (the carotid artery), as we discussed in Chapter IV.

Karen will count her pulse for only six seconds. Then she will simply add a zero to that number and have her walking-speed pulse. (Adding the zero multiplies the number by 10; since there are 10 sixes in a minute, this will give her a quick and quite accurate figure.) The reason for counting for only six seconds, other than the fact that it's easy and convenient, is that your heart rate will begin to drop soon after you stop walking. By counting for six seconds, you'll get a number that is probably exactly what you would have gotten if you could have taken your pulse while you were moving. If you were to count for a full minute, or maybe for as few as 15 seconds, your pulse would be starting to return to its resting level, and your figure would not be accurate as a walking-speed pulse.

Let us imagine that Karen does what I have described. She counts nine heartbeats in six seconds. She adds the zero and sees that her walking-speed pulse rate was 90. She repeats the whole procedure—walking at her usual pace for a couple of minutes, stopping to count for six seconds, adding the zero—and gets 80 this time. On her third try she gets 90 again; on her fourth, 80.

Apparently, 85 is about Karen's walking-speed pulse. Had her pulse turned out to be 140 instead of 85, she would already have found the correct pace for her Physical Conditioning Procedure. However, unless Karen is a person who almost never does anything but sit around or sleep, she is probably much too young at 16 years to be able to reach her Physical Conditioning pace by merely walking. (But notice that if Karen were 93 years old, and if 65 beats per minute were still her resting pulse rate, her target would be 85. Her usual walking speed would be the correct pace for her Physical Conditioning Procedure.)

Karen will next begin to jog very slowly. She will jog slowly for a minute or so, come to an abrupt halt, count for six seconds, and repeat several times. Say she gets 12 each time. Adding the zero, she sees that this slow jog raises her pulse to 120 beats per minute.

Finally, by increasing her speed to a medium-speed jog, she begins to count 14 pulses in her 6-second counting period. Now she's got it. She has found the pace that gives her about 140 heartbeats each minute. Karen is ready to start her Physical Conditioning Procedure.

She will want to move at that pace for 20 consecutive minutes, three times each week. As weeks and months go by, her heart will grow stronger. Because a strong heart does not need to beat so often (since it beats more powerfully), her resting pulse will drop a little, and her heart rate will not go up quite so fast when she exercises (or when she becomes stressed). So she will want to check herself with other six-second counts from time to time. Eventually, she will have to increase her jogging speed very slightly in order to reach her target rate. The change will be very gradual, however; as her resting pulse begins to fall to 60 or 55, her target rate will fall, too (as she does her formula to figure her target repeatedly, using her gradually revised "220-modified" figure and using her new age if she has a birthday).

Even if she finds that she is gradually moving a little faster as the months go by, she will still be just as comfortable because her body will be in better shape. Karen will be pleased with herself too, knowing that she is conditioning herself correctly and experiencing that great feeling of well-being that we get when we take proper care of our bodies. (She'll also *look* better to other people, which is not a bad feeling either.)

But I don't want you (or Karen) to forget the main point of the Conditioning Procedure. Karen will not just be in "good shape"—she will be unstressed. Unstressed, that is, compared to whatever her stress levels would be if she were not following the Physical Conditioning Procedure. If Karen is also using breathing control, muscle relaxation, self-talk-control, and so on, she will probably be unstressed compared to any of us. Even if she chooses to use no other stress control techniques, or tries to use them but is not yet very good at them, she will be unstressed compared with her former self.

Do be clear about why this has led Karen to be less stressed. Be sure you see why this is a stress control technique. We stress ourselves because of the ways in which we react to things that happen to us, or because of the ways in which we react to things we expect to have to do. The "stress" itself is our bodies' re-actions—increased heart rate, increased respiration rate, in-creased blood pressure, and so on.

Think about the Physical Conditioning Procedure. What effect will it have on those reactions? Remember what I said about Karen's heart? Her resting pulse will gradually drop; her heart rate will no longer go up so quickly when she exercises; her blood pressure will tend to behave in similar (more stable) ways; moderate activity will no longer leave her gasping for breath. Without stressing herself in the process, Karen will have built up a kind of resistance to stress.

That is why this is such a valuable stress control technique. Now Karen can be imperfect with her other techniques and still have stress reactions, but the stress reactions cannot be nearly so damaging as they were before. Now her strong, healthy heart can continue to pump at a reasonably slow rate (and her blood pressure can remain reasonably low and her breathing rate can remain reasonably normal) even when she fails to use good self-talk-control or forgets her breathing control or neglects to Count Down. When she does use those other techniques properly in addition to her Physical Conditioning Procedure, she will be a real model of stress control for the rest of us to admire.

Imagine this imaginary Karen in a classroom. Imagine, too, that she has not yet begun to use the Physical Conditioning Procedure. Imagine that her biology teacher criticizes her sharply for what the teacher thinks is carelessness on Karen's part. Picture Karen's humiliation and anger, and imagine the fight-or-flight response surging through her body. Her pulse zooms from 65 to 150 in just seconds.

Karen must sit there in class for another 30 minutes. She can't get up and run around the school building or the track. She cannot give this tremendous surge of internal activity anything to do. The adrenalin flows into her bloodstream and her pulse continues to race while her blood pressure soars. She is damaging her own body considerably, and she knows it—which may make her even more stressed than before.

Suppose that Karen is generally having a bad week—a "nervous week." No particular awful things have happened nor are expected to happen. She just feels nervous and tense. This is probably even worse than the other situation. Her pulse won't race along at 150 for the entire week, but it will probably run a lot higher than her normal 65, and so will all those other pieces of her stress reactions. Think of the likelihood of headaches, stomach upsets, and perhaps the start of a cold (as her immune system gets involved with her stress levels and can't do its germ-fighting work).

In both kinds of stressful situations, the Physical Conditioning Procedure could have made a big difference in the amount of self-damage Karen would have been doing. Had she been using the Conditioning Procedure for several months, for example, her pulse would probably not have increased from 65 to 150 when she was criticized so sharply, but only from 60 or 55 (her new resting pulse), to, say, 80 or 90. That means that her blood pressure would probably have changed very little, her respiration rate would have stayed roughly normal (even if she were not using breathing control or Counting Down), and the other pieces of her fight-or-flight response would have had a hard time getting interested in preparing her body to do something that it couldn't really do (start a fist fight with the biology teacher or run screaming out of the school building). She would have stressed herself very little despite her embarrassment and anger.

During her "nervous week," Karen's use of the Physical Conditioning Procedure would have again prevented most of those stress reactions from becoming bad enough to damage her body. Her pulse might have been slightly elevated, but it would probably still have been lower than her original normal rate of 65. Her conditioning would also have made it far less likely that her well-toned muscles would have developed aches and pains such as headaches or neck aches or backaches. Since the Conditioning Procedure generally stimulates the body toward normal digestion, Karen's stomach upsets would not have tended to occur during this "nervous week." Even further, Karen's conditioning probably would have built up her resistance to colds and other minor diseases, since her immune system would no longer have needed to become alarmed and distracted by her general nervousness.

Don't think that the Conditioning Procedure guarantees these stress control improvements. But I want you to see that, after the first few weeks of following the Conditioning Procedure, there is for most people a wide range of important changes in their bodies' stress responses.

In both kinds of stressful situations that we pictured for Karen, the Physical Conditioning Procedure could have enabled her to make it through them without much self-damage. There might have been an interesting bonus as well: If she had been following the Conditioning Procedure, and if she were to react to it like most of us, she would have found it hard to feel so terrible about the biology incident and even harder to go a whole week in a miserable frame of mind.

Why? I'm not really certain. It could be because following the Physical Conditioning Procedure makes it hard to feel bad toward ourselves for long. We succeed, you know, every time we do it! Succeeding is important to how we feel about ourselves. For most people, the world looks a good deal better at the end of a relaxing, invigorating 20-minute swim or jog or bike ride.

It's amazing how consistently this happens for most of us when we use the Conditioning Procedure.

In concluding this chapter I want to caution you about a couple of things. First, even though the formula you have used for finding your target pulse rate has been shown to be accurate, don't think that you must go that fast, especially at first. For one thing, your muscles may not be ready for 20 minutes of activity even if your heart is. One of the important reasons for using the Conditioning Procedure only three times a week is that the day(s) of rest between jogs or swims or bike rides gives your muscles time to recover. As your muscles become conditioned, they will no longer feel sore each time you begin.

If you have been inactive for a long time, even the day or two of rest may not be enough time for your muscles to recover (and that will show you in what poor shape you have let them get). Rather than doing the full 20 minutes at 70 percent of maximum heart rate for the first few times, do less than that. Even if it means 10 minutes at 50 percent, I suggest that you be careful enough with yourself so that you can enjoy the procedure even as you begin. You may find, for example, that you can feel fairly comfortable if you walk rapidly for about three minutes, then jog very slowly for one minute, then walk rapidly again for about three minutes, and so on.

If that is what it takes for you to feel comfortable, do that until your whole body gets the idea that you are actually going to ask it to *do* something at long last. Then it will quickly begin to make the internal changes necessary so that you can start working up to your 70-percent-for-20-minutes level.

One convenient way to determine whether or not you're going too fast when you first begin to follow the Conditioning Procedure is to use the "conversation test." If you are doing a walk-jog-run or a bike ride with a friend, and if you're going at a pace that is correctly nonstressful, you should be able to carry on a conversation without panting or gasping for breath or having to stop talking frequently in order to catch your breath. If you have not been active in years—notice that I said "active," not "busy" (busy people can be in horrible shape)—you should not expect to be able to get your heart to 70 percent of maximum for 20 minutes during your first few attempts. Don't try to be a hero with the Physical Conditioning Procedure. If you do, you may exhaust yourself, or suffer a minor injury in your muscles or joints, or find yourself disliking the Procedure, or all three at once. Take care of yourself. That's the purpose of stress control techniques.

I said a few pages ago that I wanted to caution you about a couple of things. I have talked about one of them. The other also has to do with taking care of your muscles.

One advantage that dancers, gymnasts, runners, and people who practice yoga exercises have over most other people is that they learn early the importance of correct stretching. Muscles require flexibility in order to be truly healthy. *Correct* stretching is seldom taught in sports or physical education classes, although I think coaches and teachers are gradually coming around to this. You should stretch *correctly* for at least a couple of minutes before and after exercising.

Do not bounce and jerk when you stretch. That can cause thousands of microscopic rips and tears in the muscle tissue. Put gentle stress on your muscles, just as I am urging you to put gentle stress on your whole body in order to condition it for the difficult stresses of living.

For example, suppose you are about to go for a walk-jog-run. Put on comfortable shoes, comfortable clothing, and then carefully stretch the muscles you'll be using. I won't go through all the stretching exercises you could do; there are many books written for that purpose. But to show you what I mean by gentle stretching, imagine that you are doing the "hurdler's stretch," seated on the floor with one leg extended straight out in front of you and the other bent so that its heel is nearly touching your hip.

Slowly lean forward until your hamstring muscle (under the thigh on the extended leg) is "on stretch"—that is, until that muscle feels tightness but not pain. Then force yourself to make that muscle relax. *Think* about it. If you do that properly, you will find that you can lean forward for another inch or two and still with no pain. Do not bounce. Hold that relaxed position for six or eight seconds. Then sit up straight. Then repeat a couple of times.

Get the idea? Gentle stretching will not rip your muscle fibers and will keep your body flexible and ready for whatever Physical Conditioning Procedure you choose. (Incidentally, this stretch-

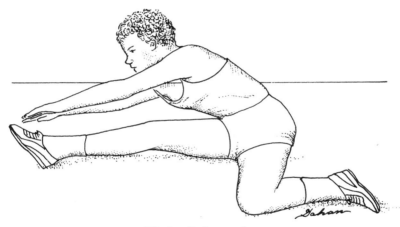

The hurdler's stretch.

ing procedure is especially important if you are lifting weights for strength and power so that you can be a better linebacker in football or a stronger center in lacrosse. Weight lifting tends to shorten your muscles as it strengthens them. The shorter your muscles, the less range of motion you'll have in your arms and legs. Good athletes are strong *and* flexible.)

I run at least 70 miles every week, usually taking only one day off from my running, so that I can do my Physical Conditioning Procedure *and* so that I can run in 26-mile marathon races. Am I doing something I've told you not to do—am I doing so much that I am stressing myself instead of conditioning myself properly to handle the stresses of living?

If you can slowly increase the amount of time you spend doing your Physical Conditioning Procedure so that your muscles remain unsore and you do not injure yourself by overuse of muscles and joints, and if you love to walk-jog-run or swim or bike ride as much as I love to run, then you can do more than 60 minutes a week of your Conditioning Procedure and still be okay. But you do not need to do any more than 60 minutes a week in order to condition yourself for stress control, and you do run a risk if you decide to do more—the risk of soreness and injury. But if you are very careful, and if you enjoy your conditioning so much that you want to spend more time at it than just an hour per week, and if you are careful (as I am) not to exceed your 70-percent-of-maximum-heart-rate level, then go right ahead. Enjoy!

Well, that's it. That's your Physical Conditioning Procedure. Quite a bit different from what "exercise" usually means, isn't it?

You can fit this in with your other stress control techniques in a variety of ways. For example, you might do your Conditioning Procedure on Mondays, Wednesdays, and Fridays and on the other days do Counting Down practice or Positive Mental Rehearsal or the Worry Exercise. But notice that Positive Mental Rehearsal could be done during the Physical Conditioning Procedure, as, to an extent, could breathing control, muscle relaxation, self-talk-control practice, and Counting Down practice. Be creative with your techniques—make your stress control techniques fit your life and your own special needs.

CHAPTER X

Stimulus Control—Stress Control Technique #7

I have considered calling this technique something other than Stimulus Control, because that term usually requires considerable explanation. But after the explaining, my students tend to prefer "Stimulus Control" to all the other names that I (and they) invent. So I'll stay with that name and do a little explaining before we start.

Dictionaries use phrases like this to define the word stimulus: ". . . any action or agent that causes an activity in an organism, organ, etc." Okay. So *anything outside you* (an action or agent) *that causes something to happen* (an activity) *inside you* (either in your whole organism or in some of the organs, such as your heart or your adrenal glands, which are part of your whole organism) *can be called a stimulus.* Stimulus Control means, then, controlling things *outside* yourself rather than *inside* yourself.

There is an important problem here, however. Remember what we learned in Chapter VI. When we discussed how to talk to yourself we took a close look at the fact that things outside you don't really cause things to happen inside you at all. We just talk that way—both to our ourselves and to other people. What really occurs is that things happen outside us (like the biology teacher scolding Karen), then we see and hear those things happening, and then *we* cause things to happen inside us *because of the way we choose to interpret those outside things.*

We say things like "He made me so mad" when we really mean *"I* made me so mad because of the way I reacted to what he said to me." (Please review some of Chapter VI if you have forgotten this vital point. You will remember that I called that chapter the most important one in the book, and I don't want you to forget my explanation there of the basic facts in stress control—the facts that show that *you stress yourself* and that, therefore, you are *in control of yourself* and of your own stress levels.)

Well, then, why am I going to talk at all about Stimulus Control, given the facts that Stimulus Control deals with changing things outside yourself and that stress and its control both happen inside yourself? That question accounts for the fact that I have saved this stress control technique until I had described the other six. I have saved it because it is the least important of the seven—because it is the only one that does not deal with changing yourself. And the only thing you can control for sure is yourself. You can never be sure of controlling other people. You can never be sure of controlling outside events, problems, and conditions—only yourself.

On the other hand, nearly every student with whom I talk about stress control has at least one thing in his or her life that is not inside that person and that ought to be changed. I never permit my students to use Stimulus Control as their only stress control technique; but nearly all my students use Stimulus Control as a small part of their overall approach to handling their stress levels. So it is worth knowing about, but it must be used in combination with your other techniques, never by itself.

Think about your own life. Are there some obvious things that occur regularly outside yourself that become stressful for you, that perhaps make no sense at all, and that could be changed without too much difficulty? For example, how about the people who drive the cars in which you ride? Do you ride to school every day with someone who drives as fast and as recklessly as possible? Is that stressful for you? Why do you do it, in that case?

Maybe you ride to school with someone who drives well but cannot leave on time. Is that stressful for you? Then why do you do it?

How about the "morning rush hour"? I don't mean the automobile traffic on the roads. I mean the human traffic in your bathroom and kitchen at home. If that is a stressful hour for you (and probably for your parents, brothers, and sisters), why not take a look at the way things are organized (or disorganized) during that hour and make some changes? I know business people whose offices are beautifully organized but who have never bothered to sit down with their families to organize their own rush hours. A little organizing can make that morning time a relaxing and enjoyable way for a family to start the day, rather than a source of stress for the whole group. Most people find their days stressful enough without having this kind of terrible beginning day after day.

What about your English class where you endure that particularly hateful teacher every day during third period? Not only do you find yourself highly stressed by the way you react to the teacher, but in your opinion the teacher does not teach very well. My preference, of course, is for you to use any or all of the first six stress control techniques to handle your stress levels in English class. But I repeat—most students have at least one thing in their lives that could be changed easily and probably ought to be—not just to reduce their stress levels but for other good reasons as well. (Other reasons? Well, you'll live longer if you do not ride in cars with crazy drivers, your family will be happier if it reorganizes its mornings, and you'll learn more English if you arrange to change to another teacher's section.)

Most of these changes require guts, don't they? Arranging to get to school without riding with your best friend—what will he or she think of you if you change? Raising the issue of the morning rush hour with your parents—what if they get angry and say that you're trying to "interfere"? Speaking with your principal about your problems with the English teacher—how will the principal react?

Those are important questions and they show again why you must become good with one or, I hope, several of the other six stress control techniques rather than just using Stimulus Control. The very act of making changes that are outside yourself often requires that you use some of the first six techniques. Are you going to have a talk with that friend with whom you've been riding to school? Then you'd better use your self-talk-control beforehand, and you'd better Count Down as you start to talk, and you'd better use muscle relaxation during the discussion.

Are you going to talk with your parents about the rush hour? You'd better calm yourself when they start to get angry by using your breathing control technique.

And how about this meeting with your principal about the English situation? If you have been using your Physical Conditioning Procedure regularly and if you practice your Positive Mental Rehearsal for several days before the appointment, you will handle the stress of making that change without damaging your own insides in the least.

You can see, then, that use of Stimulus Control does require that you have the use of at least some of your other techniques. You will need them in order to do anything of importance with Stimulus Control. There is another reason, too. Use of Stimulus Control alone could lead you simply to run away from your challenges—which is, you realize, the exact opposite of what I have been urging you to do. But to repeat, most of you probably have one or two things going on regularly that you could try to change, for stress control reasons and for other good reasons as well. If so, use your first six stress control techniques, get yourself ready, and then make those changes that you have avoided too long already.

Let us go through a detailed example of Stimulus Control use. Imagine a family consisting of the parents and three children— Marie, aged 17, Andy, aged 16, and Holly, aged 14. Andy, let's say, is in his junior year and hopes to take the Scholastic Achievement Tests next month. He very much wishes to attend a certain engineering college which, he knows, requires extraordinarily high scores on the Achievement Tests.

Four weeks before the exams Andy talks with his family at supper about the ways in which he wants to prepare for the day-long tests. He tells them that he'd like to arise earlier each morning so that he can put in, first, a half-hour of study specifically for the tests, and second, 20 minutes of Physical Conditioning Procedure on his Mom's stationary bicycle on Mondays, Wednesdays, and Fridays, and 15 minutes of Positive Mental Rehearsal on Tuesdays, Thursdays, and Saturdays. (He wants to use the stationary bike so that he can continue to read and review for the tests during his Physical Conditioning Procedure.)

These changes in his morning habits will affect the rest of the family in several ways. First, the house is quite small and the sound of his alarm clock usually awakes his sisters, whose rooms adjoin his own. So he is asking them to allow him this special favor in view of the crucial importance to him of making high scores on his tests. Next, the 20 minutes on the stationary bike will prevent his Mom's use of the bike at her own favorite time for doing the Physical Conditioning Procedure. Andy is asking her for a favor, too—that she will use the bicycle at some other time of day for this four-week period. Finally, most difficult of all, he is asking that all four family members try to be unusually quiet for 15 minutes on Tuesdays, Thursdays, and Saturdays from 6:45 A.M. until 7:00 A.M. while Andy practices his Positive Mental Rehearsal.

This is Stimulus Control. He is asking for changes in the ways in which his family usually operates each morning. As usual in Stimulus Control, he has more than one reason for asking. He has stress control reasons and other good reasons as well. Andy is, in a sense, asking his family for a gift. How would your family react to requests like Andy's if your own circumstances were as important and temporarily stressful as his are? Would your family be eager to cooperate? Or would they regard your requests as merely selfishness on your part? If Andy's sisters were to view his requests as unreasonable, what should he do?

Rather than getting angry, Andy probably ought to use self-talk-control to help himself understand his sisters' views, and then he might consider offering them some compromises. He might offer to take their turns at washing the dishes, for example, during the four weeks. Or he might give up his use of the family car so that Marie could use it more often and agree to work on Holly's broken front-wheel brake on her 10-speed bike. If the tests are vitally important to Andy, in other words, he should practice his self-talk-control enough so that he will be willing to try to see his stressors through other people's eyes, not just through his own. And in other people's eyes, their own lives usually seem just as stressful as yours or more so.

Remember that. Since stress is caused by the ways in which we all interpret what is happening or is going to happen to us (that is, by the ways in which we talk to ourselves about our stressors), you can see that it makes no sense to claim that someone else's life is not "really" as stressful as your own. If someone else sees his or her life as stressful, it *is* stressful. Their interpretation makes it so.

Andy should, then, be talking to himself about that fact before he ever approaches his parents and sisters about his efforts at Stimulus Control. He must remind himself repeatedly that what may seem completely obvious to him will not necessarily seem even remotely obvious to anyone else. Not because those other people are "bad" or "stupid" or any such thing—it is because their own lives probably look extremely stressful to them and because each of them no doubt has events approaching that to them look just as crucial as do Andy's Achievement Tests.

If Andy has prepared himself properly, he will not become stressed or angry when he encounters some resistance from his sisters. He will simply show them that he understands their reluctance, and he will offer some trade-offs until he finds the Stimulus Control arrangements he needs in order to prepare himself for the Scholastic Achievement Tests. They are too important for his future for him to give up or to add to his own stress levels by becoming upset with his family in the process of talking with them. (Incidentally, if Andy is lucky enough to have parents and sisters who enthusiastically accept his requests without demanding any compromises, he has truly been given a gift by them, hasn't he? In those circumstances I think it would be great if Andy did something nice for them after the tests are completed—maybe a small gift for each of his sisters and some flowers for his Mom, since those are the three people who have been directly affected by his Stimulus Control changes. Marie and Holly might not look pleased by that—they might just look embarrassed—but inside we all are warmed by someone's efforts to thank us for something we've done for them.)

I think this is all the explanation you need in order to begin using the techniques of Stimulus Control. It's a simple technique to describe and to talk about. Maybe that's why I'm so afraid that people will misuse it. Used by itself, as your only way of dealing with stress, it could become a terrible thing—a way to hide from the world and to avoid every challenge or discomfort you face. For that reason I have given it to you only after carefully presenting six other good, strong stress control techniques, any of which can be used by itself or in combinations to enable you to face your challenges or discomforts without fear (and with increased chances of success). Use this seventh technique with caution and in combination with the other six. In that way Stimulus Control can help you face up to some needed changes in your daily life—changes that you probably should have made long ago.

CHAPTER XI

A Final Step: Your Contract with Yourself

After I have worked with a student (or adult) for some time, I usually ask him or her to make a contract for me to inspect as a sort of "final exam." Before I am willing to say that a student clearly understands how to put stress control techniques into daily use, I want to see a written statement that shows which techniques are going to be used, how and how often they are going to be practiced, how the student will judge his or her progress, and so on.

It's not that I may "flunk" someone on this Self-contract. Not that at all. But I think you will find that putting something down on paper (and maybe showing it to someone else) will force you to be clear about your problems, your goals, and the techniques you will use to confront them. This Self-contract is designed to be (1) an outline for you to follow, and (2) a promise to yourself. Not a promise to me. A promise that you make to you!

The Self-contracts my students write are part of a five-step procedure that goes like this:

1. Self-diagnosis
2. Assessment of commitment
3. *Self-contract*
4. Weekly contract review
5. Quarterly contract rewriting

These steps are quite simple. To do the Self-diagnosis, merely keep a log or diary for about three weeks. Divide each page down the middle, and each night before going to bed write down on the left side of the page those things that stressed you during the

day. On the right side of the page write down your "stress reactions" to each one. Sometimes the right side of your page may
look somewhat like the list I supplied back in Chapter III, but
often it will not, because most of your reactions will not have
been that strong. Frequently your right-hand notes will say things
such as "butterflies in stomach off and on during the whole
morning," or "laughed and giggled like a little kid throughout
the party," or "chewed my fingernails all through the lecture."

Enter everything in the left column that could possibly have
been stressful for you. Nothing is too small or insignificant to be
included. The idea, remember, is to help yourself "diagnose"
your own stress problems. Often my students are surprised after
three weeks of log-writing to find certain things showing up in
the log over and over—things they weren't aware of at all
Things in both columns that they had simply not focused on
before.

For example, sometimes a student (I'll imagine a female) will
come to see me when her log is completed and say something
like this: "You know, I really love my boyfriend and we don't
have many fights, but more than half the entries in my stress log
are about him. I'm really surprised at how often I've listed 'irritability' and 'inability to concentrate' in my right column, and
those entries are nearly always paired in the left column with
something my boyfriend did or said."

That doesn't mean, of course, that she needs to rush out and
break up with him. But it does mean that the two of them may
not be talking to each other very "sanely" (as we discussed in
Chapter VI), which probably also means that she (and he) need
to review that chapter on how to talk to yourself and this time
put those self-talk ideas to work.

Set up your log in whatever way you think it will be of most
value to you. (Table I shows an example of the way I suggest.)
The aim is to get a clear picture of what things are stressing you
and of your typical stress reactions. With that information about
yourself, you can move to Step two in the procedure. (One reminder: Your stressors and stress reactions will not always be

TABLE I
A Sample Stress Log

Wednesday, March 5

1. Continued to worry about talking with the coach about missing practice next Monday
2. Late for 4th-period class—sent to office to get a late slip
3. Thought about my embarrassment over 4th-period lateness several times during the afternoon—thought about the dumb way I had looked, getting so red in front of everybody
4. Talked to coach about missing practice next Monday

5. Dad angry at me for my lateness to class 4th period—said I'd have extra chores Saturday

1. Unable to concentrate on classes all morning

2. Embarrassed! Face got red, heart pounded, started to perspire
3. Tight feeling in stomach—hard to concentrate on classes again—anger at myself—muscles tense in face and stomach

4. *Really* tight in stomach—voice trembled—face got red again, heart pounded, perspired a lot
5. Started to get mad but did some good self-talk and a little breathing control and had no noticeable reaction

Thursday, March 6

1. As soon as I woke up started worrying about how I'll do in tomorrow night's game

2. Called on to read in French class—did a fair job

3. In afternoon study hall, got more nervous than ever imagining how I'll do in the game
4. Unable to go to sleep—constantly thinking about the game

1. Headache by 2nd period—no concentration on classes for second day in a row—butterflies in stomach—tightness in stomach, head, and shoulders
2. Heart pounding right away—face red—afterwards headache got worse
3. Had to go to the bathroom—headache *really* bad now

4. Diarrhea now—headache continues

neatly paired together; sometimes, for example, your stress reaction to an entire day of dozens of stressors may simply be a single one such as "generally nervous all day" or "more and more depressed as the day went on." Usually, however, there are specific reactions to specific stressors, and we can learn to be sensitive to them.)

The second step, Assessment of Commitment, means that,

when you have looked carefully at the two columns in the log, you will have enough information about yourself and your stressors to decide how much time and effort you should devote to stress control. Does your Self-diagnosis show that you have no regular (daily) stressors at all and that your reactions to the stressors you do encounter are insignificant? Such as "smiled at the teacher's silly comments and went back to my work—completely forgot about the incident until Jim asked me what had happened." Or such as "thought about the upcoming game several times during the day—each time with a feeling of relaxed confidence and anticipation; I'm certain I'll play well and enjoy the competition." Or such as "felt a momentary twinge of anger when I saw my grade, because Mr. Brown never did mention that he wanted us to use the other textbook—but I understand the material really well, so I'm sure I'll get my grade up there where I want it."

If those are the only sorts of items you find when you review your stress log, then your Assessment of Commitment should probably result in a big zero. In other words, if you're already handling your stressors beautifully, why make a commitment to practice and use stress control techniques? You may still want to be familiar with these techniques so that you can select one (or several) when you eventually do feel some stress building up (such as with Andy's Scholastic Achievement Tests) or when one of your close friends asks you what he or she might do to handle daily stressors. But your log would be telling you plainly that you need no special commitment to stress control right now in your life.

Few of you, of course—very few, in fact—will find your log as "perfect" as the one I just imagined. Almost all of you will find that you do need at least some commitment to stress control. When you study your log and Assess the Commitment your stress levels deserve, you may well find yourself realizing that you ought to make a fairly strong commitment. Maybe the Worry Exercise for breathing control and muscle relaxation for five minutes each morning, Counting Down practice for five minutes at bedtime, the Physical Conditioning Procedure three times weekly, and a couple of major Stimulus Control steps.

You may find that your stress centers around a certain repeated event, such as your team's twice-a-week soccer contests. If so, maybe your commitment should be to do Positive Mental Rehearsals each night when you get home after practice, focusing on your performance against the next opponent.

Assess your Commitment by looking thoughtfully at your Self-diagnosis log. Then write your Self-contract, which is the third step. Write your Contract in the way that makes most sense to you. Take time to look carefully at Table II, which shows a sample Self-contract designed to be followed for three months.

Notice how much different from each other the three sections under Part III will have to be in this example. The Stimulus Control section (III C) is something that will be done only once. The Counting Down/Breathing Control/Muscle Relaxation section (III B) will require two minutes of practice each night and will probably be effective immediately. But the Positive Mental Rehearsal/Self-Talk-Control section (III A) will demand 10 minutes of daily practice and yet will probably not be noticeably effective for several weeks. By then, improvement should be evident.

Don't assume that the Self-contract will magically make you into an unstressed person. Certain kinds of goals (as with II-A in the sample) will demand weeks or months of persistent effort. Others (as with II-C) can be reached in a day. Either way, putting your problems, goals, and plans for dealing with them on paper will force you to be clear to yourself about the steps you need to take. Your Self-contract is to be your plan of attack *and* your promise to yourself.

Many of my students like to add one other thing to their Self-contract after they have worked out its three sections to their satisfaction. They like to do what is done with certain "real" contracts and other official documents—sign it and have it witnessed by two people. That usually means that they go to two

TABLE II
A Sample Self-contract

For three-month period starting ——————— and ending ———————:
I. Most Important Stressors
   A. Sports (games, not practices)
   B. French class (translating passages aloud, usually once or twice each class period)
   C. Supper (Dad quizzing me about my "performance" at school and at practice)
II. Stress Control Goals
   A. To learn to look forward to playing in ballgames rather than to be scared I'll fail to do well—to eliminate pregame headaches, diarrhea, and inability to concentrate on school work
   B. To learn to relax about French class—to reduce my fight-or-flight reaction to being called on to translate
   C. To change Dad's supper habits—to get him to change the way he talks to me at supper
III. Stress Control Techniques
   A. For Sports . . . . . .
      1. Positive Mental Rehearsal
      2. Self-Talk-Control

Strategy: For five minutes at bedtime and five minutes after I wake up each morning—Positive Mental Rehearsal in which I picture myself doing well in the game, picture myself looking forward to the game and picture myself using good self-talk-control while I do those mental pictures ("I won't make me scared when I think of the game. . ." and "I won't make myself tense my stomach and head muscles when I think of the game. . ." and *"I will expect to do well in the game. . .")*

   B. For French Class . . . .
      1. Counting Down
      2. Breathing Control
      3. Muscle Relaxation

Strategy: After my evening five minutes of Positive Mental Rehearsal for Sports, I will do Count Down practice for two minutes—I will Count Down toward both breathing control and muscle relaxation—and when I am called on in class I will Count Down before speaking and use breathing control and muscle relaxation while translating

   C. For Supper . . . . . .
      1. Stimulus Control

Strategy: Since I have so much trouble talking seriously to Dad, I will write him a letter explaining how hard it is for me to enjoy supper and have good digestion when he quizzes me every time. I'll ask that he allow me to give him a report on how my day went after supper is over and the cleaning up is finished friends or teachers and ask that they look over the Self-contract. These friends or teachers ("witnesses") watch while the student signs at the bottom and then add their own signatures as official observers of the seriousness of the Contract writer's commitment.

For many of you, this may be an important thing to do when your Self-contract is completed. Some of you will not want that step. But showing your Self-contract to two people whom you respect can often add to your own level of motivation—can make you more determined than you would otherwise have been to reach the stress control goals you have laid out for yourself.

The fourth step in this procedure is your Weekly Contract Review. That means exactly what it says. Once a week you will reread your Self-contract as a reminder of its exact wording and as a way of reviewing your previous week's stress control work. How did you do? Did you do precisely what you committed yourself to doing? If not, why not? You have written down exactly what you've decided you must do, but little improvement will occur unless you practice doing those things.

The final step in the procedure is the Quarterly Contract Rewriting. If you selected the best techniques to use to fit your own situation when you first wrote your Self-contract, in three months (one quarter of a year) you will see progress, and usually a lot of it. After that length of time it is time to decide how to move on. If all your original Self-contract goals have been met, you may want to select a new set of more difficult goals to work toward. You may prefer to do another three-week Stress Log first, in order to see what differences there may be in your stressors and your current reactions to them.

If your goals have not been met at all, one of two things must have occurred. Either you failed to use the techniques and technique-practices that you promised yourself you would, or you selected techniques that did not fit well into your situation. If the second was the problem—selection of the wrong techniques for your life—you will want to do a Quarterly Contract Rewriting for that reason. If the first was the problem—you simply failed to do what you promised yourself to do—no rewriting may be needed. You will merely want to ask yourself seriously whether or not your stresses are important enough to you (and to those around you who are affected by your stressed behaviors) for you to want to do anything about them. So far, the answer to that would apparently have been No.

As you'll remember from our look at how to talk to yourself, however, that does not mean that your answer cannot be changed to Yes. It is not that you "cannot" do something like this or that you "have no self-discipline." It is that you "have not yet" done something like this or that you "have not yet started to behave in ways that people call 'disciplined.'" Confucius is usually credited with having said that "a journey of a thousand miles begins with a single step." Take the first step in putting your Self-contract into practice. Do it for just one day. Then the second day will be a little easier and the third a little easier still. Eventually you will have some new habits—and nothing is so easy to do as something that has become a habit.

That is the five-step procedure that most of my students use after they have gained a clear understanding of each of the stress control techniques. Most of them get a lot of satisfaction out of understanding their own bodies and minds better, and then out of watching themselves change to meet the goals they have written out for themselves.

Often my students become very creative with their Self-contracts, especially after working through their original three-month Contract. The experience they gain from the first one helps them do a better job with the second and often leads them to dream up techniques or practices that are ingenious combinations of those I have written about or completely new twists on the use of practice of a particular technique.

One of many examples I could give you of this kind of creativity is that of my son when he was 12 years old and first trying to do something about his frequent headaches. I talked to him about muscle relaxation, thinking that would be the most effective way for him to teach himself not to be faced with so much pain so often. But eventually Barry said to me, "Dad, that muscle relaxation idea didn't work very well for me. But what is working is this—I just don't think about anything more than five hours before it's going to happen!"

Without my having talked to him about it, then, Barry had started to use a little self-talk-control.

The point is that this exact way of doing self-talk-control was not a way that I would have recommended. It prevents certain kinds of planning, for one thing; it could be a way of ignoring a real problem, for another; and it's very hard for most people to do, for still another. But it was creative, it apparently fit into my son's situation at that time, and it was working—he was having fewer headaches. That's what I meant when I said that often my students dream up new ways of using or practicing their techniques. The idea, after all, is to learn to handle your stressors successfully, not necessarily to do one or several of these techniques exactly the way I have suggested. The best approach for most of you will probably be to use these techniques at first in the ways I have described but then to modify them as you grow more confident and skilled with your stress control.

I am excited to think that many of you who have now read to the end of this book are not yet 20 years old. I know from daily experience (and from doing and studying physiological research) that any stress control steps that you learn to put into your life now are likely to have important and lasting effects upon your chances of living a healthful, successful life. I know that, having read this far, it must be clear to you that hiding from stress is never the best way to handle it. The goal is, rather, to learn to use techniques so that the stresses of life no longer damage your insides, no longer frighten you, and no longer prevent your performing as well as you should in school, at work, in athletics, and so on. In the process you will have freed yourself to face your challenges with enthusiasm and confidence.

I find myself smiling when I imagine young people learning to face stress with assurance. I am led to picture a whole generation of young people moving into adult life ready and eager for its goods and bads, its peaks and valleys, its stresses and distresses.

A whole generation of young people free from constant reliance on pills for headache, on pills for "nerves," on pills for stomach disorders—and most important of all, free from being held back and trapped by the limitations which, except for their stress control techniques, they probably would have gradually begun to place upon themselves.